READING IN SECONDARY CONTENT AREAS:
A Language-Based Pedagogy

Zhihui Fang and Mary J. Schleppegrell

WITH CONTRIBUTIONS FROM ANNABELLE LUKIN, JINGZI HUANG, AND BRUCE NORMANDIA

Ann Arbor

THE UNIVERSITY OF MICHIGAN PRESS

ISBN-13: 978-0-472-03279-2

2011   2010   2009   2008   4   3   2   1

PREFACE

This book describes a new approach to secondary content area reading. The approach, called **functional language analysis,** goes beyond the strategies often recommended—vocabulary, text structures, key words, and personal responses—to offer teachers explicit ways to focus on language itself to help students comprehend and critique the advanced texts of secondary schooling. Based in functional linguistics, the book provides a meaning-based metalanguage for talking about text that enables students to learn content at the same time they are developing advanced literacy skills.

The book is intended primarily for teachers and teacher educators of core secondary subjects (science, social studies, mathematics, and language arts). Reading teachers and literacy coaches in middle and high schools will also find it valuable. The book leads the reader through analysis of texts in different subjects to illuminate the challenges students face in reading those texts and to offer ways of engaging students in exploring meaning in text. It provides detailed suggestions for incorporating language analysis and exploration of meaning into classroom instructional practices to develop students' reading proficiency in content areas. The book is also a resource for language and literacy scholars who conduct research on reading, language, and literacy in academic content areas, as it offers ways of evaluating texts and analyzing the meanings they present. The book can be used in content area reading courses, in graduate seminars on literacy education and applied linguistics, and in professional development workshops and institutes.

We are grateful to Annabelle Lukin, Jingzi Huang, and Bruce Normandia for their contributions to the book. We also thank the many colleagues, friends, and students who have provided valuable comments on earlier drafts of the chapters in this book. They include Mariana Achugar, Thomasenia Adams, Anne Curzan, Luciana de Oliveira, Anne Gere, Gloriana Gonzalez, Stacey Greer, Tracy Linderholm, Kerry McArthur, Stephen Pape, John T. Rowntree, Jenny Sealy, Megan Sweeney, and Ebony Thomas. Finally, we acknowledge with appreciation the support of Kelly Sippell of the University of Michigan Press.

CONTENTS

chapter 1

Language and Reading in Secondary Content Areas

Not only is language at the centre of all transmission of educational knowledge, whether arts, social science, natural science or technology, but…as one moves across from one subject area to another language is likely to be functioning in rather different ways.

—Halliday, 2007a, p. 295

Secondary school teachers today are challenged to engage an increasingly diverse student body in learning specialized and complex subject matter. At the same time, students are often poorly prepared to read the texts that present disciplinary knowledge. This book offers middle and high school teachers new language-based strategies for helping students read advanced texts with greater understanding and engagement. It introduces **functional language analysis,** an approach that enables students to read closely and critically and develop an understanding of how language works in different subjects. It describes the particular features of texts in science, history, mathematics, and language arts and offers strategies for talking about these features in ways that connect with the curricular goals in those subjects.

CHALLENGES FOR SECONDARY TEACHERS

Many adolescents are unable to read the often dense and complex texts of secondary school subjects and are not prepared for the challenges they will face in college and workplace reading. More than eight million students in Grades 4–12 are struggling readers, and 26 percent of eighth

1

graders and 23 percent of twelfth graders are unable to demonstrate an overall understanding of what they read, with fewer than one-third of eighth and twelfth graders reading at levels necessary for school success (Perie, Grigg, & Donahue, 2005). In some secondary schools, as much as 75–80 percent of the students struggle with academic texts (Carnine & Carnine, 2004). Poor and ethnic minority students, as well as those for whom English is not the primary language, are heavily and disproportionately represented among struggling adolescent readers. For example, only 4 percent of eighth grade English language learners are reading at grade level or higher, compared to 31 percent of all eighth graders (Short & Fitzsimmons, 2007).

Few secondary teachers have the expertise needed to help their students develop "advanced literacy" (Schleppegrell & Colombi, 2002) in curriculum content areas. In a recent report, Berman and Biancarosa (2005, p. 8) note:

> Often middle and high school teachers view themselves as content specialists. They sometimes ignore the problems of their struggling readers or compensate for them by giving students notes from a reading assignment or reading a text aloud instead of helping students learn to extract information from a text themselves. These teachers do not have the training or knowledge to do more, and they are often frustrated that remediation services are less available and less effective for their struggling adolescent students than they are for struggling younger readers.

This and other reports (e.g., Alvermann, 2001; Biancarosa & Snow, 2004; Heller & Greenleaf, 2007; IRA & NMSA, 2001; Moore, Bean, Birdyshaw, & Rycik, 1999; NCTE, 2004, 2006) underscore the need to continue reading instruction in the secondary school. They also suggest that secondary reading instruction should go beyond basic skills and strategies—such as phonological awareness, phonics, and fluency—that are typically emphasized in the elementary school. Recognizing that every content area has its own characteristic literacy practices, these reports call for the development of subject-specific reading skills among adolescents, urging secondary teachers to incorporate literacy strategies into subject matter teaching.

Biancarosa and Snow (2004), for example, suggest that teachers emphasize "the reading and writing practices that are specific to their subjects, so students are encouraged to read and write like historians, scientists, mathematicians, and other subject-area experts" (p. 15). Similarly, the National Council of Teachers of English (NCTE) recognizes that

> the academic discourses and disciplinary concepts in such fields as science, mathematics, and the social studies entail new forms, purposes, and processing demands that pose difficulties for some adolescents. They need teachers to show them how literacy operates within academic disciplines. In particular, adolescents need instruction that integrates literacy skills into each school discipline so they can learn from the texts they read. (2006, p. 5)

The NCTE (2004) further suggests that teachers of adolescents receive support and professional development that enable them to "teach literacy in their disciplines as an essential way of learning in their disciplines" and "create environments that allow students to engage in critical examinations of texts as they dissect, deconstruct, and re-construct in an effort to engage in meaning making and comprehension processes" (p. 3). Standards for middle and high school literacy coaches, charged with the responsibility of helping secondary teachers understand the demands of literary, mathematics, science, and social studies texts, also emphasize discipline- specific reading strategies (IRA, 2006). Recommendations for English language learners suggest that these students need to engage in instructional practices that simultaneously support academic literacy development and content area learning, including interacting with text, asking and answering text-based questions, and focusing on text structures and discourse features of different types of texts (Meltzer & Hamann, 2004, 2005).

The key to developing discipline-specific reading skills and strategies is in understanding how knowledge is presented in characteristic patterns of language in each subject. This book prepares teachers for this important work by offering an approach to secondary content area reading that engages students in analyzing the ways language constructs knowledge in science, history, mathematics, and language arts. The approach, called **functional language analysis,** provides a way of talking about language that enables readers to better understand the texts they read and to engage with the purposes and values of the disciplines they are being apprenticed into.

SPECIALIZED LANGUAGE IN THE SECONDARY SCHOOL

Students do not learn to read once and for all in the elementary years. Elementary school reading cannot fully prepare readers for the literary works, historical documents, scientific explanations, and mathematical problems that challenge secondary school students (Fang, 2008). We learn to read the kinds of texts we practice and engage with, and each of the subject areas of secondary schooling confronts students with texts constructed in patterns of language they are unlikely to have encountered in the texts they read in the early grades. As they move into secondary school, students engage in new contexts of learning that are further removed from their personal lives and everyday contexts. The texts they are expected to read regularly often deal with specialized topics that are different from the typical subject matter of reading materials in the elementary grades. As the knowledge students engage with becomes more formalized and complex, so too do the patterns of language that construct that knowledge (Christie, 1998; Halliday, 1993; Schleppegrell, 2004). These patterns are not just complexities that construct barriers to privilege "insiders." Instead, they are functional and necessary for enabling the accumulation of knowledge and advancement of a field.

Advanced disciplinary knowledge requires specialized language, as complex meanings cannot be conveyed with precision in everyday language. Secondary-level science, social studies, language arts, and mathematics use patterns of language that enable these disciplines to develop theories, to engage in interpretation, and to create specialized texts. These patterns of language, or **grammar**, are the focus of this book. We use the term *grammar* not to refer to a set of rules for correctness, but instead to focus on the systems of the English language that are resources for meaning making.

Let's take a look at the kind of reading this book addresses. This passage from a tenth grade history textbook (Beck, Black, Krieger, Naylor, & Shabakam, 2003, p. 423), for example, comes from a section analyzing the causes of the Great Depression:

> By 1929, American factories were turning out nearly half of the world's industrial goods. The rising productivity led to enormous profits. However, this new wealth was not evenly distributed.

This passage has technical words that situate it in economic history (e.g., *productivity, profits*). But the challenge for students is not just in the vocabulary. Students also need to recognize the way the authors have packaged the information to build from sentence to sentence. *The rising productivity* refers back to the point in the previous sentence that *by 1929,*

American factories were turning out nearly half of the world's industrial goods. Enormous profits are recast in the following sentence as *this new wealth.* Sentences in history texts are typically constructed to present and then repackage new information, and students can learn to recognize this common pattern of information flow.

A focus on language can also help students recognize the point of view being presented, an aspect of critical reading. The sentence *However, this new wealth was not evenly distributed* suggests that the historian may be raising concerns about the growth in productivity and profits. The conjunction *However* signals this change in focus, and in fact the next paragraphs of the text develop the problems that arose from the uneven distribution of wealth. Another aspect of historical interpretation is the attribution of agency and cause. As even this brief passage shows, the language of history texts at the secondary level often attributes agency to abstractions such as *this rising productivity* or to non-human actors such as *factories.* Understanding that there are real historical actors behind these abstract or institutional agents and considering the perspective that the abstraction offers help students recognize how implicit or explicit interpretation is always present in history texts.

In science, the language patterns that construct reports, explanations, and expositions are also distinct from those that construct everyday knowledge and from those that construct other subjects, as this excerpt from a sixth grade science textbook (*Science Voyages,* 2000a, p. 558) illustrates:

> The cells that line the nasal cavities have cilia, tiny hairlike extensions that can move together like whips. The whiplike motion of these cilia sweeps the mucus into the throat, where you swallow it.

This short excerpt contains technical vocabulary (e.g., *cells, nasal cavities, cilia, mucus*) that constructs specialized content. Two long noun groups, *the cells that line the nasal cavities* and *tiny hairlike extensions that can move together like whips,* allow the author to pack a large load of information into the first sentence. *The whiplike motion of these cilia* in the second sentence is a rewording of *cilia...can move together like whips* in the first sentence. This grammatical repackaging turns a verb, *move,* into an abstract noun, *motion,* which is then further modified with *whiplike,* an adjective that is itself repackaged from the noun *whips.* By restating what is presented in the first sentence and making it the point of departure for discussion in the second sentence, the author is able to elaborate on the function of the cells that line the nasal cavities. This way of structuring text creates a discursive flow that facilitates scientific reasoning, but it also challenges students to understand densely organized information. Learning how to work with students to reveal the meanings in these complex language patterns can help teachers achieve their curricular goals more effectively.

In mathematics, the language patterns that construct word problems are also distinctive, as illustrated in this example from a high school calculus textbook (Anton, 1992, p. 509):

> At time t = 0, a tank contains 4 lb. of salt dissolved in 100 gal. of water. Suppose that brine containing 2 lb. of salt per gallon of water is allowed to enter the tank at a rate of 5 gal./min. and that the mixed solution is drained from the tank at the same rate. Find the amount of salt in the tank after 10 min.

An obvious feature of this word problem is that it uses language, mathematics symbolism (e.g., numbers, the equation), and mathematical expressions (e.g., *rate* expressed as *gal/min*). Mathematics texts typically draw on meaningful configurations of language, mathematics symbolism, and visual display (e.g., graphs, diagrams), and students must be able to make sense of the ways these different systems interact. They also need to recognize the language features that indicate what a mathematical text is asking them to do. This calculus text, for example, directs the students to *suppose* and to *find* in solving the problem. It contains both specialist language (e.g., *at a rate of, brine, per gallon*) and everyday words that assume specialized meanings (e.g., *at, suppose, solution, find*). Long, complex noun groups, such as *4 lb of salt dissolved in 100 gal of water* and *brine containing 2 lb of salt per gallon of water,* have to be recognized as constructing entities that need to be manipulated in some way to solve the problem. Everyday meanings such as "salt and water are mixed together" and "how much salt" are constructed here in abstract noun groups as the *mixed solution* and *the amount of salt,* respectively. This repackaging of meanings is a common means of creating mathematical concepts to be manipulated and transformed in problem solving. Finally, passive voice constructions such as *is allowed to enter* and *is drained* enable the writer to maintain a focus on the flow of water rather than on the person who performs the acts, but this representation can be alienating and difficult for students to understand. These features of mathematical language make mathematics word problems challenging, but teachers can address these challenges through explicit discussion of the language features and how they can be analyzed in solving the problems.

In literary texts, language is a creative and artistic resource. Language patterns of all kinds are made use of by writers to entertain, divert, challenge, and educate readers through literary texts. Secondary school students read poetry, drama, essays, and fiction and engage with authors from different time periods, cultures, and literary styles. The patterns of language they are expected to read expand dramatically as they explore literary themes. When students study more complex literary texts in secondary school, there are many opportunities to explore the use of language patterns for aesthetic ends. Take, for example, this excerpt from Chapter 3 of Jane Austen's (1818/1998, pp. 22–23) *Persuasion:*

> "Then I take it for granted," observed Sir Walter, "that his face is about as orange as the cuffs and capes of my livery."
>
> Mr. Shepherd hastened to assure him, that Admiral Croft was a very hale, hearty, well-looking man, a little weather-beaten, to be sure, but not much, and quite the gentleman in all his notions and behaviour; not likely to make the smallest difficulty about terms, only wanted a comfortable home, and to get into it as soon as possible; knew he must pay for his convenience; knew what rent a ready-furnished house of that consequence might fetch; should not have been surprised if Sir Walter had asked more; had inquired about the manor; would be glad of the deputation, certainly, but made no great point of it; said he sometimes took out a gun, but never killed; quite the gentleman.

As Leech and Short (1981, pp. 325–326) explore in their discussion of the representation of speech and thought in literary texts, the speech of Sir Walter is given in the full direct speech form, which establishes him as a man confident of his place in the world. By contrast, Mr. Shepherd's speech is of an indirect kind; that is, it is reported and not quoted by the narrator. In addition, it is truncated, creating the sense of a man falling over himself to get everything said. While the passage is a third person narration, the narrator is channeling the character by adopting his style of speech—indeed, by virtually quoting directly the words of Mr. Shepherd—and in so doing, brings the reader into a more intimate relationship with the character. Thus, Mr. Shepard is depicted as a deferential, inexhaustible man—a man trying to persuade himself rather than Sir Walter.

This passage from Austen is one small illustration of linguistic patterning for literary effect. When students can explore patterns of this kind in literature, they can go beyond impressionistic or intuitive evaluations of a literary text. At the same time, they are engaged in learning about what language is like and how it is structured.

The language patterns that construct these academic texts draw on the grammatical systems of English in different ways from those used in everyday informal interactions. They also vary from one subject to another. The history and science textbooks we have quoted represent knowledge that has been recontextualized for educational purposes, drawn from professional (or disciplinary) discourses. The text of the mathematics word problem attempts to contextualize mathematical knowledge in a situation that students can visualize or relate to, but at the same time embeds mathematics content that has to be understood in abstraction from any particular context of situation. The language of a literary text recreates life's experiences, but it does so in ways that allow artistry, allusion, and the embedding of universal human themes. Each discipline, then, confronts students with texts that draw on different sets of language features to construct content knowledge in distinctive ways. It is for this reason that Unsworth (2001, p. 11) has argued that "it is no longer appropriate to talk about 'literacy across the curriculum.' Instead there is a need to delineate 'curriculum literacies,' specifying the interface between a specific curriculum and its literacies rather than imagining there is a singular literacy that could be spread homogeneously across the curriculum." This notion of multiliteracies motivates the work in this book as we illustrate what is characteristic of different school subjects through analysis of how the English language is used in the texts students read. We provide strategies for talking about language and text that respond to the goals and purposes of each subject and offer teachers and students new ways of engaging with text.

This focus on language offers a complementary approach to activities that enable teachers to create effective contexts for learning and to engage with students' backgrounds and prior knowledge. Current approaches to content area reading typically recommend teaching students to predict, clarify, visualize, and summarize; make connections and inferences; ask questions; do think-alouds; look for key ideas in the text; use graphic organizers; take notes; or skim and scan (e.g., Deshler, Ellis, & Lenz, 1996; Fisher, Brozo, Frey, & Ivey, 2007; Vacca & Vacca, 2005). These strategies are valuable, but many of them assume students can already make sense of the dense, complex language in academic texts. Functional language analysis goes beyond—and adds to—these strategies by providing tools for deconstructing texts, sentence by sentence, to help students process unfamiliar discourse patterns and talk about how meaning is constructed through language choices. This gives students the language analysis skills needed to effectively utilize other reading strategies, enabling them to engage with content more deeply and critically.

CONTENT AREA TEACHERS AND READING INSTRUCTION

To succeed in secondary schooling and beyond, students need to develop specialized literacies relevant to each content area as well as a critical literacy that they can use across content areas to engage with, reflect on, and evaluate specialized and advanced knowledge. Teachers play an important role in apprenticing their students into disciplinary knowledge and practices. To do this, they need to develop expertise for helping students engage with the texts of their discipline. Text is the primary medium through which disciplinary knowledge is produced, stored, communicated, and critiqued; as a result, text reading constitutes an integral part of disciplinary practices in our society. This makes an emphasis on reading and text in content learning appropriate and neces-sary. Scientists, mathematicians, historians, novelists, and other special-ists regularly read the professional literatures in their fields, and they do so with care, critical-mindedness, and healthy skepticism. Without text and without reading, it is practically impossible for them to engage in the social practices that constitute their disciplines. Likewise, to learn the content of different subject areas and to engage in disciplinary prac-tices, students need to develop the ability to read (and write) the texts of these subjects.

Engaging all students as readers and writers across subject areas is also a matter of social justice. For their own personal development and for effective participation in a democratic society, students need to be able to read with comprehension and critically evaluate the texts they encounter. They need to read and reason with texts of varying types and complexities and to engage with knowledge that in today's world transcends national and cultural borders.

Reading proficiency develops when students are able to see how language works in text, and learning to see this comes through interac-tion with experienced readers who can make the meaning and structure available to the novice. Content area teachers—teachers of science, social studies, mathematics, and language arts—are subject matter experts and rightly focus their attention on the subject matter knowledge to be developed by their students. But while knowledge about the content to be taught is a prerequisite for good teaching, being an expert in the discipline is not enough. Teachers also need knowledge about how to make the content available to students, and teachers who can talk with students about both the structures and the meanings of the texts can better engage students and help them learn content more effectively.

As content specialists, secondary teachers are also typically "good readers" in their subject areas, familiar with the patterns of language that construct the texts they read and teach. They understand the meaning without even being aware of the linguistic challenges. For secondary school students, on the other hand, the patterns may not be familiar. The knowledge they are struggling to learn is presented to them in texts they often perceive as dense and abstract, with technical language and complex structure that can be alienating and challenging. Attention to this language and how it works in different subjects can help students develop content knowledge at the same time they develop more advanced reading skills. Explicitly showing students how to read advanced texts can be a part of teaching every middle and high school subject and at the same time can enhance disciplinary learning. As teachers of specialized subject matter, secondary school teachers are best positioned to help students recognize the specialized ways language works. The functional language analysis approach presented in this book provides a meaning-based metalanguage teachers can use to talk with students about the texts they read and offers concrete strategies that enable teachers to be explicit about how language works to present complex, technical, and abstract knowledge in their content areas. The approach supports content learning at the same time it helps students develop advanced literacy skills.

FUNCTIONAL LANGUAGE ANALYSIS

Functional language analysis is based in systemic functional linguistics (SFL), a theory of language that provides a framework for demonstrating how meaning is constructed in particular language choices (see, for example, Eggins, 2004; Lock, 1996; Schleppegrell, 2004; and Thompson, 2004 for accessible introductions to the theory). SFL sees language as a resource for making meaning in the same way that color is a resource for painters to create artwork. We make different kinds of meaning for different purposes and contexts by drawing on the different options that language affords, just as painters use different combinations of colors from their palette to create different effects with their paintings. Developed by linguist Michael Halliday in the past 40 years (e.g., Halliday, 1978; Halliday & Matthiessen, 2004) and used by educators and researchers around the world, SFL provides the foundation for the pedagogical principles and ideas in this book and enables us to describe the linguistic features of texts in different subject areas by showing how those features enable the text to mean what it does.

The meaning that we are concerned with is of three kinds: the **experiential meaning** (what a text is about), the **interpersonal meaning** (the interaction, interpretation, attitudes, and judgments embedded in a text), and the **textual meaning** (how a text is organized as a coherent message). Every use of language, whether spoken or written, involves saying something about the world (the experiential meaning), enacting a social relationship of some kind (the interpersonal meaning), and presenting a message in a coherent way (the textual meaning). In fact, each **clause** constructs meanings of all three kinds, contributing to the overall meaning constructed in a text.

The clause is the basic element of a text, and this book helps students recognize how these three kinds of meaning are simultaneously constructed in the grammar of each clause. From the point of view of experiential meaning, students will learn to recognize **processes**, constructed in verb groups, **participants**, constructed in noun groups, **circumstances**, constructed in prepositional phrases and adverbs, and **conjunctions** that link clauses. From the point of view of interpersonal meaning, students will learn to recognize that each clause constructs a relationship between the author and the reader or among the characters in the text through the **mood system,** which allows us to make statements, ask questions, and issue commands, as well as through the **modality system,** which enables us to express evaluative meanings related to possibility, usuality, obligation, and inclination. And students will learn to recognize how each clause constructs textual meaning as it begins from a particular point of departure and moves to present something new, using the system of **Theme/Rheme** structuring.

This three-dimensional focus on language—on how experiential, interpersonal, and textual meanings are constructed in the language—draws attention to the knowledge and values of a discipline and so helps us focus on subject-specific ways of making meaning and the patterns of language that are typical of the texts in each subject area. The functional linguistics terms are a meaning-based metalanguage that is developed in the following chapters as we illustrate how meanings of all these three kinds are relevant to text comprehension and composition in all content areas. Throughout, we show how readers can apply functional language analysis as they use the metalanguage to explore texts in meaningful ways.

Functional language analysis offers practical strategies for supporting students' engagement with text through detailed analysis of language and accompanying discussion about the meanings of the language patterns. The approach provides a way of talking about language that enables teachers and students to recognize language patterns that are typical and functional in the texts of different content areas. Using functional language analysis, students simultaneously learn **through** language and **about** language, better understanding content at the same time they gain a better understanding of the language used to construct that content. By helping students see how meaning is presented through language in their disciplines, teachers enable students to become independent readers who can reflect in critical ways on what they read. Functional language analysis also offers teachers strategies for evaluating the difficulty of reading materials and the quality of students' writing (Fang, 2005a, 2005b, 2006; McKenna, 1997; Schleppegrell, 1998). It has helped secondary teachers support students' reading development (Hammond, 2006; Schleppegrell & de Oliveira, 2006) and expository writing development (Schleppegrell, 2005; Schleppegrell, Greer, & Taylor, 2008), evaluate what makes a text more effective (Macken-Horarik, 2006; Mohan & Slater, 2004), and improve students' academic language performance (Boscardin & Aguirre-Muñoz, 2006).

OVERVIEW OF THIS BOOK

This book presents concrete strategies for reading and analyzing texts in four core secondary school subject areas—science, history, mathematics, and language arts. Each chapter illustrates new ways of engaging students with texts to enable their participation in learning, and each chapter offers linguistic strategies for helping students recognize how different language choices present specialized, abstract, and multilayered meanings. As a whole, the book presents a comprehensive approach to analyzing and interpreting texts that addresses the key linguistic challenges associated with the development of advanced literacy in curriculum content areas.

We begin with science in Chapter 2 by analyzing the three kinds of meaning through a focus on the noun group in science texts. The noun group is a key structure in all uses of language (Fang, Schleppegrell, &

Cox, 2006), but in science it takes on particular functional loads. Noun groups of varying complexities enable scientists to create technical taxonomies, construct scientific theories, transcategorize processes and qualities, distill everyday experiences, expand information, combine pieces of argument for logical reasoning, embed perspectives and ideologies, and provide cohesive linkages within a text. We illustrate how the technicality and abstraction of science texts are revealed in the way that noun groups are typically used to put the focus on experiential meaning. We introduce functional metalanguage terms for talking about the elements of the clause as processes, participants, and circumstances. We show that sometimes processes or qualities are realized in noun groups as nominalizations and describe the role of nominalization in the formation of a cohesive text as it enables information to flow and reasoning to develop. We also demonstrate how abstract and depersonalized nouns enable scientists to embed ideology and scientific values in their writing, part of the interpersonal meaning in science texts. We then show that it is the complex noun group that accounts for the density of information in science texts. We introduce the strategy of analyzing Theme/Rheme structure to focus on textual meaning and show how scientists often use movement from Rheme to Theme to present scientific information and develop arguments. These functional language analysis strategies enable teachers and students to explore how the technicality of science interacts with other features of science discourse—abstraction, density, and tightly knit structure—to develop sequences of logical reasoning and scientific worldviews.

In history, two key challenges for students are recognizing the interpretation that is always present in history texts and recognizing how time and cause interact as the historian presents a reconstruction of events. Students are often asked to identify causes and effects in history or to recognize how particular events and actors influenced other events and actors. Having tools for recognizing how authors construct these time-cause relationships gives students power in adopting similar tools themselves or in critiquing the choices authors have made. In Chapter 3, we introduce the notion of four kinds of processes **(doing, saying, sensing, being)** to enable discussion of experiential meaning—that is, discussion about what is happening in the text. This is linked to interpersonal meaning as we discuss how the perspective of the author is presented in participants in the clause and in the way reasoning is made explicit or left implicit. These features are part of the interpretation an author infuses into any text about history. We also focus, from a textual perspective, on how the text is organized, analyzing how time and cause are constructed by looking at clause Themes and recognizing sequencing through time, construction of moments in time, and rhetorical structuring that explicitly explains historical events through thesis-driven arguments. We describe the changing patterns in textbook passages as events are chronicled, historical debates are reconstructed, and explanations that interpret history are provided, identifying the language features that can be analyzed to explore these patterns.

Mathematics teachers sometimes think that language is less relevant to them and may dismiss the notion that attention to language would be important. In Chapter 4, Jingzi Huang, a language educator, and Bruce Normandia, a mathematics educator, collaborate in bringing linguistics and mathematics together to show the importance of language in comprehending and solving word problems in algebra and geometry. They illustrate how attention to patterns of language can help students identify what a problem is asking them to do, what key information is provided, and what mathematical concepts and operations are relevant. They show how solving word problems requires simultaneous engagement with language, mathematics symbolism, and visual display, focusing on the key role that language comprehension plays in this engagement.

Chapter 4 illustrates the analysis of experiential meaning in showing how recognizing processes, participants, and circumstances can help students identify key information provided in a word problem and the mathematical entities to be manipulated in solving it. The analysis of clause mood is introduced to offer tools to identify what the reader is directed to do in a word problem, an aspect of interpersonal meaning, as the author of a word problem questions or commands the reader. The chapter also highlights some textual meanings in word problems through analysis of references, ellipsis, and conjunctions that reveals what needs to be recovered by the reader for full understanding. These analyses help identify some of the linguistic challenges involved in reading word problems, and an approach to unpacking the language of algebra and geometry word problems is presented that can also be applied to other mathematics texts.

Language arts teachers are aware of the importance of language in their discipline, but few of them have been introduced to a meaning-based grammar for talking about language itself in systematic ways that can help students engage in principled interpretation of literary texts. Chapter 5, by Annabelle Lukin, presents linguistic tools for exploring meaning in literary texts. Lukin, who is a linguist based in Australia (where the functional language analysis approach was first developed), suggests that grounding the interpretation of literature in concrete analysis of language helps "overcome the purely private nature of literature as a school subject, where the pupil is left guessing as to what reaction to a particular work the teacher expects of him" (Halliday, 1982, p. 12). She illustrates how the key themes in a literary work can be brought to the foreground through systematic analysis of language at different levels—graphology, word, grammar, and rhetorical organization.

Chapter 5 presents a comprehensive language analysis of experiential, interpersonal, and textual meaning and also introduces analyses of graphological and sound patterns to reveal important features of a poem's structure and rhetorical organization. Experiential meanings are illuminated through the analysis of the processes, participants, and circumstances to show who is engaged in doing, sensing, saying, and being; key motifs in a literary text are revealed through analysis of lexical and referential chains. The notion of interpersonal meaning is developed through an analysis of mood that focuses on speech functions, showing how two characters in a poem interact with each other. In addition, the role of modality in presenting meanings about possibility, certainty, obligation, and other features of interpersonal meaning is introduced. From the point of view of textual meaning, the chapter shows how analyzing Theme helps us see what the author takes as the point of departure for each clause and which characters' voices are foregrounded.

Language arts is rich with texts and text types, but the analysis of a poem in Chapter 5 illustrates the depth of insight that can be gained through systematic exploration of language from a functional perspective. While some literary genres such as novels or plays may not lend themselves to comprehensive analysis of a whole text, students can use the functional approach to analyze language at key moments in a text, to analyze the kinds of processes different characters engage in throughout a work, to look at how an author represents different characters in language, and to explore how the author colors the text with language choices of various kinds.

In Chapter 6, we review the metalanguage that we have developed throughout the book and show how it relates to more traditional ways of talking about grammar. We then offer suggestions for incorporating functional language analysis into regular instructional activities. Literacy development and content learning are intrinsically linked, so students' reading ability can develop along with their content knowledge if teachers have strategies for enabling students to learn grade-level content through a functional focus on language. Chapter 6 describes how developing students' understanding about the ways grammatical resources are used to construct meanings in different school subjects can be an integral part of secondary reading pedagogy as teachers focus explicitly on how language works in their respective fields. Through this work, teachers can make visible the knowledge and values of their discipline and engage students in examining texts critically. The activities we suggest also enable students to interact with text in collaborative ways as they engage in discussion about how language constructs knowledge and ideology. In addition, we suggest how this functional approach can be applied to other key areas of literacy instruction in support of content learning, as it gives teachers tools for conducting reliable assessments of text difficulty and quality, guiding student writing development, and supporting cross-disciplinary and schoolwide curricular collaboration.

As we explain how meaning is built in language by looking at particular texts, we see how language works in different subjects. The kinds of meanings that are in focus are relevant to that subject, but the language analysis strategies can also be used across subjects in exploring different kinds of texts. Teachers can benefit from reading all chapters and not just the one related to their particular subject, as each chapter offers something different that can be applicable and valuable to other content areas as well. While each discipline has its own set of textual practices and ways of using language, and while each chapter highlights those practices and the particular ways that language constructs knowledge, teachers may see connections across subjects as they read about the texts of other disciplines. Discussion as to why a particular subject uses language in ways that are similar to or different from other subjects can engender deeper understanding and stimulate further inquiry. Teachers may also recognize that there are some kinds of texts in their field that are similar to those presented from other subjects. We invite teachers to find connections across disciplines and engage with the worlds of other subjects to find that their own subject area is illuminated in this process. Toward this end, we also provide a study guide in the Appendix to facilitate discussion and exploration of the chapters in the book.

Reading secondary school texts is hard, and it takes time to develop reading proficiency in a range of subjects. Many students get little experience with academic ways of using language outside of school, so they need explicit focus in the classroom on the ways language varies and makes meaning in the texts of secondary school subjects. The content area teacher is best placed to develop this explicit focus. This book offers teachers a new and powerful way of teaching secondary reading that supports the development of discipline-specific literacies in content area classrooms. As teachers help students see how language is used in the particular texts and contexts of their subject areas, students simultaneously learn the content presented in these challenging texts and become proficient in using language to read and write in the ways expected in the disciplines. By embedding language analysis in content area reading instruction, teachers support deeper learning of content at the same time they provide their students with tools for advanced learning.

chapter 2

Technicality and Reasoning in Science: Beyond Vocabulary

There are practical reasons for analyzing scientific texts. The most obvious is educational: students of all ages may find them hard to read, and…the difficulty is largely a linguistic one. So if we want to do something about it we need to understand how the language of these texts is organized. Of course, if a text is hard to read the difficulty is bound to be in some sense linguistic…: but in the case of scientific writing it seems that there are certain features of the way meanings are organized, and the way they are 'worded', that present special problems for a learner, over and above the unfamiliar subject matter and its remoteness from everyday experience.

—Halliday & Martin, 1993, p. 124

Many secondary school students find science texts challenging and avoid reading them. An informal survey of U.S. high school students (Guzzetti, Hynd, Skeels, & Williams, 1995) found that two-thirds to three-fourths of the students never or rarely used textbooks except to complete assigned problems. Other studies have reported similar findings, suggesting that secondary students engage in very little reading of any published text about science in school (Wellington & Osborne, 2001). When students do read science textbooks, they often need instructional support that is seldom available (DiGisi & Willett, 1995; Schumm, Vaughn, & Saumell, 1992).

One of the reasons students find science texts difficult and alienating is that school science uses language in unfamiliar ways. While some science textbooks may be poorly written or "inconsiderate" (Jones, 2006;

Kesidou & Roseman, 2002), even well-written school science texts use language patterns that sound foreign to students. To help students cope with this unfamiliarity, teachers typically focus instruction on scientific terminology. However, the difficulty of science lies not just in technical vocabulary, but more broadly in the grammar, as "it is the total effect of the wording—words and structures—that the reader is responding to" in reading a text (Halliday & Martin, 1993, p. 71).

Science is a specialized discipline with its own ways of making meaning. Scientific advances over the past few centuries have widened the gap between the specialized knowledge of science and the commonsense knowledge of everyday life (Reif & Larkin, 1991). These advances have given rise to new ways of using language to deal with abstract phenomena and concepts and to communicate scientific principles, processes, and arguments. This "scientific language" has evolved for functional reasons to meet the needs of scientific methods, theory, and argument (Halliday & Martin, 1993). At the same time, however, it also makes science challenging and inaccessible to many students.

Veel (1997) has likened students' movement through school science to a linguistic journey through the history of science. In the early years of scientific inquiry, the most common texts that scientists wrote were recounts of experimental procedures and descriptions of results. These are also the kinds of texts typically written in the elementary grades, and they call for language that represents experience in direct ways ("this is what we did and this is what we found"). As science developed, it also developed new ways of using language. As scientists write complex reports, explanations, and discussions that engage debate about scientific phenomena, they need to present and argue for their findings, using language that constructs abstractions and theoretical entities. In so doing, they have produced specialized ways of using language that we recognize as "scientific." Similarly, in secondary school science, students also have to engage with more complex and abstract language to read and write the texts of advanced science topics. It is for this reason that science educators Wellington and Osborne (2001) have declared: "One of the major difficulties in learning science is learning the language of science" (p. 1).

Reform initiatives in science education (American Association for the Advancement of Science, 1993; National Research Council, 1996; Rutherford & Ahlgren, 1990) emphasize performance-based activities that favor the "sciencing cycle" of conducting an observation; recognizing a problem; formulating a hypothesis; designing an experiment; collecting, analyzing, and interpreting data; and arriving at a conclusion.

This movement toward "doing science" has helped stimulate students' interest in science and foster their scientific habits of mind. However, Kamil and Bernhardt (2004) caution that "the emphasis on doing science could lead one to assume implicitly that language is unimportant or a nuisance factor and that evidence of science learning can be generated effectively by nonlanguage methods or performance assessment" (p. 131). They argue that reading science texts should be made an integral and more prominent part of school science.

A scientific theory is, in essence, "a linguistic construal of experience" (Halliday & Martin, 1993, p. 8). More emphasis should, therefore, be given to the (written) language of science in science teaching and learning. As science educators Norris and Phillips (2003) have argued, a conception of science literacy must account for the essential role of text in the advancement of science. A focus on the ways language is used to communicate scientific inquiries, procedures, and understandings can enhance students' science reading competence, enabling them to access important realms of scientific knowledge and values.

THE GRAMMAR OF SCIENCE

The language of science is simultaneously technical, abstract, dense, and tightly knit—features that contrast sharply with the more interactive and interpersonal language of everyday spontaneous speech and of reading materials for beginning readers. This language plays a central role in the construction and representation of scientific knowledge, processes, and worldviews. It enables scientists to define, describe, explain, theorize, classify, catalogue, and analyze natural phenomena, as well as to reason, critique, and argue for/against a particular hypothesis, theory, or viewpoint. It is, in short, "a means of engaging with and constructing science understandings and an end in that it is also a record of this engagement" (Hand & Prain, 2006, p. 103). This suggests that learning science entails learning the organization and logic of scientific ways of using language. Functional language analysis offers teachers concrete strategies for helping students better understand and use the language of science, promoting the development of science literacy and scientific habits of mind.

Our exploration of the language of science begins with its most obvious feature, **technical vocabulary.** But technical terms occur in phrases, sentences, and discourses of definition, explanation, and reasoning; so talk about words quickly leads to consideration of how scientists use particular patterns of language. Science texts use **abstraction** to create theoretical entities and technical taxonomies in building scientific theories;

they use **high density** in packaging meaning to facilitate presentation of information, and the information they present is in **tightly knit structures** to create a cohesive flow of discourse. These four features—technicality, abstraction, density, and tightly knit structure—are prominent in an excerpt from *Genes & DNA* (Walker, 2003), an award-winning title for Grades 6–8 from the 2004 list of Outstanding Science Trade Books for Students K–12 compiled by the National Science Teachers Association in cooperation with the Children's Book Council. The excerpt is presented in Figure 2.1. Three widely used science textbooks—*Science Voyages* (2000b) for seventh grade, *Modern Biology* (2006) for ninth and tenth grades, and *Conceptual Physics* (Hewitt, 2002) for high school—also offer examples of these four key features of scientific language.

WORDS WITH SPECIALIZED MEANINGS: SCIENTIFIC LANGUAGE IS TECHNICAL

Science aims to construct a non-commonsense interpretation of the physical world, and to do so, it uses two types of technical vocabulary, each of which presents comprehension challenges to students. The first type of technical vocabulary consists of words that are specifically coined for and unique to science. They include **naming words** (e.g., *trachea,*

FIGURE 2.1
Text Excerpt from *Genes & DNA* (Walker, 2003, p. 25)

DNA: The Molecule of Life

A time span of 50 years is insignificant compared to the billions of years that life has existed on Earth. But the 50 years between 1953–2003 are of incredible significance to biology because it was during that half of a century that many of the secrets of life were revealed. The trigger for these revelations was one of the great science feats of all time—the discovery of the structure of DNA, the material from which genes are made. Once DNA's structure was known, scientists were able to figure out how it provides a library of instructions that control the cells that make up our bodies and those of all other living things. At the beginning of this century, the Human Genome Project made another great leap forward by completing the enormous task of reading the letters that make up the instructions contained in our DNA. This achievement marks the start of a process that one day will allow humans to understand completely how DNA makes us all human beings but also makes us unique individuals.

chromosome, cerebellum), **classifying words** (e.g, *rhodophyta, arthropoda, omnivore*), **process words** (e.g., *hybridization, photosynthesis, refraction*), and **describing words** (e.g., *androgynous, deciduous, nocturnal*). These words typically contain prefixes, roots, and/or suffixes of Greek or Latin origins (e.g., *phagocytosis = phago + cyt + osis*). They are essential to science in that they encapsulate many of the key concepts of the discipline. Without them, science would be incomplete, inaccurate, and imprecise.

The second type of technical vocabulary is **everyday words with technical meanings.** These words are usually familiar to students; however, when used in science texts, they often take on specialized or metaphorical meanings that are different from their vernacular senses. Words like *fault, sponge, solid, factor, frequency, force, matter, medium, charge, positive,* and *volume* belong to this type. For example, the word *medium* in *a medium-sized drink* means "average, neither large nor small," but in the science context it can mean "a substance through which something is carried or transmitted," as in, *In which <u>medium</u> does sound travel the fastest?* This type of word can be at least as problematic to the reader as the first type, even though it appears perfectly simple and decodable.

Genes & DNA, in Figure 2.1, explores the basics of genes and their wide-ranging functions as the code for life. In this text, words such as *genes, genome, cell, DNA,* and *biology* belong to the first category of technical vocabulary. Words that belong to the second category include *library, instruction,* and *read.* Together, these two types of words construct specialized meanings that enable the study of genes and DNA.

Technical words like these contribute to the **experiential meaning,** or content, of a text. They are typically highlighted (in bold) and defined in the glossary of a book. They are often the focus of vocabulary exercises and quizzes in class. However, when there is a heavy concentration of such words in a small chunk of text, students can feel overwhelmed and lose interest in reading. In Text 1, for example, there are ten technical words (italicized) in the 23-word sentence. With technical vocabulary accounting for more than 40 percent of the total words, the sentence is difficult for students to process.

Text 1: *Phylum Rhizopoda* is composed of the *protozoans* called *amoebas* that use *pseudopodia, extensions* of their *plasma membrane,* to move and *engulf prey.* (From *Modern Biology,* 2006, p. 551)

When a science text contains a high proportion of technical words such as these, it can be difficult to comprehend, as the meanings of these words are often inaccessible to or poorly understood by students (Cassels & Johnstone, 1985). Because of this, it is important to develop students' awareness of technical vocabulary and engage them in using these words in multiple ways as they learn new scientific concepts.

WORDS THAT INCORPORATE PROCESSES AND QUALITIES: SCIENTIFIC LANGUAGE IS ABSTRACT

Technical words are important to the building of scientific theories. They participate in scientific explanation and reasoning not only as things (nouns), processes (verbs), and qualities (adjectives), but also as entities that incorporate processes or qualities (abstract nouns). Abstract nouns are a valuable linguistic resource because they help scientists repackage information in ways that enable the development of a theory. One way that scientific information can be repackaged is through the grammatical vehicle of **nominalization**. Nominalization involves turning processes, as expressed by verbs like *distill*, or qualities, as expressed by adjectives like *sensitive*, into nouns (e.g., *distillation, sensitivity*). Traditional grammar defines nouns as persons, places, or things. But the things of everyday life are often quite different from the things that are represented in the nouns that commonly appear in science texts. The nouns of science are often **abstractions**, words that have to be understood as abstract things that also incorporate the processes or qualities they are derived from. Nominalization is a key resource for turning processes or qualities into grammatical things, and this has value for building a science text and developing arguments.

In *Genes & DNA* (see Figure 2.1), for example, the abstract nouns *discovery, significance, instruction, beginning, revelation,* and *achievement* are derived from verbs or adjectives:

VERB/ADJECTIVE		ABSTRACT NOUN
discover	→	discovery
significant	→	significance
instruct	→	instruction
begin	→	beginning
reveal	→	revelation
achieve	→	achievement

These "de-verbal" and "de-adjective" nouns enable the author to synthesize what has already been said, creating entities that can participate in scientific reasoning as nouns and allowing for more flexibility of expression. The author of *Genes and DNA* characterizes *a time span of 50 years* as *insignificant,* but then calls the time between 1953 and 2003 *of incred-*

ible significance, making *significance* a noun so that it can be modified as *incredible.* At the same time, however, these nominalizations also make the text more abstract because they embody processes or qualities that readers may have to unpack in order to understand. *These revelations,* for example, has to be connected with *many of the secrets of life were revealed* in order to make sense of the passage.

Text 2 also has a pattern of processes being reconstrued, in this case, as technical abstractions:

> Text 2: Cells divide in two steps. First, the nucleus of the cell divides, and then the cytoplasm divides. Mitosis is the process in which the nucleus divides to form two identical nuclei. Each new nucleus is also identical to the original nucleus. Mitosis is described as a series of phases or steps. The steps are named prophase, metaphase, anaphase, and telophase. . . . (From *Science Voyages,* 2000b, p. 532)

The process in which the nucleus of the cell divides and forms two identical nuclei is recast as a technical term, *mitosis.* In getting technicalized, it has also become condensed and thus more abstract, as the two-step division that the term refers to is no longer obvious. But as a noun, this new theoretical entity now readily lends itself to further classification. *Mitosis* can be assigned to classes (e.g., animal cell mitosis, plant cell mitosis) and can carry *attributes* (e.g., it consists of four different phases, which are prophase, metaphase, anaphase, telophase). At the same time, it functions as the anchor point for further discussion of the topic on cell growth and division. This, in effect, allows scientists to build a theory of cell reproduction.

As these examples demonstrate, nominalization typically involves synthesis, condensation, abstraction, and technicalization of the language of everyday life. In everyday language, processes are typically presented in verbs, qualities in adjectives, and things or entities in nouns. By presenting processes and qualities in nouns, scientific language reconstrues these processes and qualities in ways that enable them to participate in grammatical formulations that construct dense explanations and abstract reasoning. Thus, highly nominalized texts can present a significant challenge to comprehension at the same time they are functional for scientific reasoning. Multiple nominalizations may also be present in a single sentence, as shown in Text 3 (e.g., *nuclear fission, the delicate balance, the attraction of nuclear strong forces, the repulsion of electric forces*):

> Text 3: Nuclear fission involves the delicate balance between the attraction of nuclear strong forces and the repulsion of electric forces within the nucleus. (From *Conceptual Physics*, Hewitt, 2002, p. 630)

One nominalization can even be embedded within another to form complex noun groups, as shown in Text 4 (e.g., _experimental verification of Einstein's explanation_ of _the photoelectric effect_, _the direct proportionality of photon energy to frequency_).

> Text 4: Experimental verification of Einstein's explanation of the photoelectric effect was made 11 years later by the American physicist Robert Millikan. Every aspect of Einstein's interpretation was confirmed, including the direct proportionality of photon energy to frequency. (From *Conceptual Physics*, Hewitt, 2002, p. 598)

An additional comprehension challenge for students is that information is typically lost in the process of nominalization. Nominalization enables the suppression of the actor and/or the object that is being acted upon, and so has the potential to create ambiguity. For example, in Text 3, *the repulsion of electric forces* could mean "electric forces repulse something" or "something repulses electric forces." Students have to draw on their knowledge about nuclear fission to decide which interpretation is more plausible, and understanding how nominalization works can help students think about the possibilities.

Environmental texts in science often capitalize on the power of nominalization to suppress the social agents responsible for environmental problems and, in doing so, often obscure causation. In Text 5, for example, nominalizations such as *loss of habitat*, *lost vegetation*, and *reduced vegetation* distill the process of cutting down trees in the rain forest without subsequent replacement into abstractions that conceal the parties (e.g., people, companies, institutions) who are responsible for deforestation and, thus, for habitat loss and reduced vegetation.

> Text 5: Some land is used as a source of wood. Trees are cut down and used for lumber, fuel, and paper. Often, new trees are planted to take their places. In some cases, especially in the tropical regions shown in Figure 16-8, whole forests are

> cut down without being replaced. Each year, 310,000 km² of rain forest disappear worldwide. It is difficult to estimate, but evidence suggests that up to 50,000 species worldwide may become extinct each year due to *loss of habitat*. Organisms living outside of the tropics also suffer because of the *lost vegetation*. Plants remove carbon dioxide from the air when they photosynthesize. The process of photosynthesis also produces oxygen that organisms need to breathe. Therefore, *reduced vegetation* may result in higher levels of carbon dioxide in the atmosphere. Carbon dioxide is a gas that may contribute to a rise in temperatures on Earth. (From *Science Voyages*, 2000b, p. 452)

The omission of social actors allows the text to focus on the happenings in the environment without naming the ultimate human culprits. Non-human agents (e.g., *trees, new trees, whole forests, rain forest, organisms, plants, species, carbon dioxide*) and abstract entities (e.g., *evidence, the process of photosynthesis, reduced vegetation*) are used instead as grammatical participants in the processes (e.g., *are cut down, disappear, suffer, become, contribute to*) that culminate in land use and other environmental problems. These non-human agents and abstract entities also participate in the processes (e.g., *are planted, replaced, remove, result in, produce*) that create potential solutions to the environmental problems. In order to understand who the ultimate responsible parties are, what they have actually done to create environmental problems, and what can be done to solve these problems, students need to be able to unpack these abstract concepts; and to do so, students need to recognize the way nominalizations are strategically deployed in this text.

As Text 5 shows, by using non-human agents and abstract entities, the text obscures the real causes of, as well as eventual solutions to, the land use problem. This way of using language, as Chenhansa and Schleppegrell (1998) have demonstrated, can impede students' full comprehension of environmental texts and discourage their active involvement in solving environmental problems. Helping students recognize these patterns of language use enables them to read more critically and to see the way particular points of view are presented.

Nominalization, then, is a powerful grammatical resource that contributes important **experiential, interpersonal**, and **textual** meanings to the discourse of science. It allows scientists to create technical taxonomies, to synthesize and systematize detailed information, to build theories, to embed ideology and value, and to develop a cohesive chain of reasoning (Halliday, 1998; Veel, 1997). Therefore, while nominalization makes science texts more abstract and difficult to read, it is also necessary for constructing the kind of knowledge that science represents.

PACKING NOUN GROUPS INTO CLAUSES: SCIENTIFIC LANGUAGE IS DENSE

Not only do nouns enable scientists to transform processes into technical taxonomies and abstract entities that can carry attributes and participate in scientific processes, they also enable scientists to pack a heavy load of information into sentences, resulting in dense texts that are taxing to process and comprehend. To explore the effect of informational density on the readability of science texts, we can calculate and compare the **lexical density** of different texts by analyzing how much information they pack into each clause. The **clause** is the basic unit of organization in language, and sentences are made up of one or more clauses. Each clause includes a **process**, expressed in a verb of some kind, and may also include one or more **participants**, expressed in noun groups. In addition, a clause may also include one or more **circumstances**, typically realized in adverbs or prepositional phrases, as in:

PARENCHYMA CELLS	ARE FOUND	THROUGHOUT A PLANT
participant	process	circumstance
noun group	verb group	prepositional phrase

The terms *process, participant,* and *circumstance* are part of the language of functional grammar that allows us to focus on meaningful chunks of language and not just on individual words. Identifying the processes helps a reader recognize how many different clauses, or goings on, are presented in a sentence. There are different kinds of clauses. Typically each clause contributes something new to the evolving text, but not every clause can stand alone. Sometimes a clause functions as part of another clause, and it is called an **embedded clause**. Consider this example:

> *A pattern of evolution in which distantly related organisms evolve similar traits is called convergent evolution.*

In this sentence, the definition of *convergent evolution* includes two processes expressed in verbs: *evolve* and *is called*. But the sentence has only one main clause, *A pattern of evolution is called convergent evolution.* The embedded clause, *in which distantly related organisms evolve similar traits*, does not function independently, but instead serves to identify the particular *pattern of evolution* that is being defined. There are other patterns of evolution that might be defined in different ways. Recognizing when a clause is embedded in another clause is an important skill in reading scientific texts because the embedded clause often functions as part of a larger noun group to define or identify a key concept.

The lexical density of a text can be calculated by dividing the number of lexical items by the number of non-embedded clauses in the text. Lexical items are content words, including nouns (e.g., *gene*), verbs (e.g., *provide*), adjectives (e.g., *insignificant*), and some adverbs (e.g., *completely*). They contribute to the informational density of a text. The higher the number of lexical items per non-embedded clause, the heavier the informational load and the denser the text. *Genes & DNA* in Figure 2.1 (p. 21) has 85 lexical items in ten non-embedded clauses, yielding a lexical density of 8.5. According to Halliday and Martin (1993), the number of lexical items per non-embedded clause is about two for everyday spontaneous speech and four to six for written language; however, in scientific writing, this number can go up considerably, often exceeding ten. For example, some clauses in *Genes & DNA*, such as *At the beginning of this century the Human Genome Project made another great leap forward by completing the enormous task of reading the letters that make up the instructions contained in our DNA*, contain as many as 17 lexical items (underlined). When lexical density is this high, it can overload the reader's short-term working memory (Miller, 1967), putting strains on text processing.

The density of *Genes & DNA* is achieved primarily through the use of long, complex noun groups such as:

- the billions of years that life has existed on Earth
- a library of instructions that control the cells that make up our bodies and those of all other living things
- the enormous task of reading the letters that make up the instructions contained in our DNA
- the start of a process that one day will allow humans to understand completely how DNA makes us all human beings but also makes us unique individuals

These lengthy noun groups enable the author to pack a large quantity of semantic data into the clause structure, resulting in high informational density of text.

In English, a simple noun like *spot* can be expanded into a complex noun group such as *those two tropical rain forest hot spots in South America that have not been completely explored* by adding both pre-modifiers and post-modifiers. The structure of this long noun group can be analyzed and labeled as follows:

PRE-MODIFER	those	two	tropical	rain forest	hot
	pronoun	number	adjective	noun	adjective
	which one?	how many?	what kind?	what kind?	what is it like?
HEAD	spots				
	noun				
	what is it?				
POST-MODIFIER	in South America		that have not been completely explored		
	prepositional phrase		embedded clause		
	where is it?		which one?		

Pre-modifiers are presented in pronouns, numerals (or ordinals), adjectives, and nouns. **Post-modifiers,** on the other hand, are presented in prepositional phrases and embedded clauses. It is the combination of these grammatical resources, particularly the embedded clause, that allows a noun to be expanded almost indefinitely. The longer the noun group, the more information it holds. For example, in *a library of instructions that control the cells that make up our bodies and those of all other living things*, the head noun *library* is modified by a prepositional phrase (*of instructions*), which is itself further modified by an embedded clause (*that control the cells*). This embedded clause includes another embedded clause (*that make up our bodies and those of all other living things*), which modifies *the cells*. These multiple layers of modification and embedding, while enabling the adding of information into the clause, pose a significant obstacle to comprehension.

Because of the noun's potential for expanding, it is a particularly useful grammatical resource for providing definitions of scientific terms and for facilitating the development of arguments. Vande Kopple (1994) has shown that professional scientific discourse has a tendency to use very long noun groups, especially in the subject position of a sentence, in order to be precise and concise as well as efficient and progressive in presenting information and building arguments. This is contrary to everyday spontaneous speech, where shorter and simpler nouns (e.g., pronouns) are typical (Eggins, 2004). Texts 6, 7, and 8 illustrate the roles that long noun groups (italicized) play in the discourse of science.

Text 6: An automobile engine is *a machine that transforms chemical energy stored in fuel into mechanical energy*. (From *Conceptual Physics*, Hewitt, 2002, p. 116)

Text 7: *The series of changes in the female reproductive system that includes producing an egg and preparing the uterus for receiving it* is known as the menstrual cycle. (From *Modern Biology*, 2006, p. 1002)

Text 8: Most bony fishes have external fertilization and development. *This type of external reproduction in fishes and some other animals* is called spawning. (From *Modern Biology*, 2006, p. 795)

In Text 6, the long noun group is used to define *an automobile engine*. It contains an embedded clause [[*that transforms chemical energy [...] into mechanical energy*]]. Within this embedded clause lies another embedded clause [(*that is*) *stored in fuel*]. This multiple embedding enables the author to pack into one noun group a large amount of information that would otherwise have to be expressed in several clauses: *An automobile engine is a machine. It transforms chemical energy into mechanical energy. Chemical energy is stored in fuel.* Note that this more ordinary rendition sounds less elegant and precise and may be even more difficult to understand, as the source of the chemical energy is not immediately provided.

Similarly, in Text 7, the subject of the sentence is 21 words long. This lengthy noun group packs a large quantity of information into the sentence structure through the use of a prepositional phrase (*of changes in the female reproductive system*) that includes an embedded clause (*that includes producing an egg and preparing the uterus for receiving it*). In Text 8, the use of an 11-word noun group (*This type of external reproduction in fishes and some other animals*) as the subject of the second sentence enables the author to pick up what has been stated in the previous sentence—*Most bony fishes have external fertilization and development*—so that more can be said about it.

These examples demonstrate that long, complex noun groups with pre- and post-modifications enable scientists to pack a large load of information into the clause structure. This expanding power of nouns contributes to the informational density of a text and can increase the cognitive demands of text processing. At the same time, these expanded noun groups facilitate presentation of information and development of cohesive chains of reasoning in science texts.

THE FLOW OF CLAUSES IN TEXT: SCIENTIFIC LANGUAGE IS TIGHTLY KNIT

In science, accuracy and precision are emphasized not only in conducting experiments, but also in using language (Yore, et al., 2004). Scientists need to make coherent, organized arguments in order to convince the scientific community of the validity of their claims. To accomplish this, scientists typically introduce a concept, say something about it, and then recapitulate or synthesize what has been stated, often using a complex noun group or nominalization as the departure point for further discussion. In *Genes & DNA* (see Figure 2.1, p. 21), for example, *these revelations* is used to summarize what is stated in the previous sentence, that is, *many of the secrets of life were revealed*, so that it becomes the starting point of subsequent discussion on the topic. Similarly, *this achievement* allows the writer to synthesize what is presented in the previous sentence, that *the Human Genome Project made another great leap forward*, into an abstract entity that becomes the departure point for ensuing discussion.

This tightly knit structure of science texts, an aspect of **textual meaning**, can be explored further by analyzing clause **Themes** and **Rhemes** and the development of information through Thematic progression. The term *Theme* (with a capital *T*) is not used here in the same sense as *theme* (with a lower-case *t*), a term that is often used in the discussion of literary work (see also Chapter 5 for a discussion of this distinction). Theme (with a capital *T*) is a functional linguistics construct that helps us explore how a clause in English is organized as a message. **Theme** is "the element which serves as the point of departure for the message; it is that which locates and orients the clause within its context" (Halliday & Matthiessen, 2004, p. 64). The remainder of the message, the part of the clause in which the Theme is developed, is called the **Rheme.** Thus, the Theme can be identified with the first experiential element (most often, though not always, a noun or noun group) in a clause; the Rheme is the remainder of the clause.

In written English, a clause is typically structured in such a way that what the writer takes as already established in the text or context comes first, in the Theme, and what the writer wants to present as the point appears at the end, in the Rheme. Text 9 provides an example of this in a brief report about fish:

> Text 9: <u>Fishes</u> have eyes that allow them to see objects and contrasts between light and dark in the water as well. <u>The amount of vision</u> varies greatly among fishes. <u>Some fishes that live in areas of the ocean where there is no light</u> may have reduced, almost nonfunctional eyes. (From *Modern Biology*, 2006, p. 796)

This text consists of three main clauses (with Themes underlined). The Theme of the second main clause, *the amount of vision*, builds on what is presented in the first clause as the description of the type of eyes that fishes have (*eyes that allow them to see objects and contrasts between light and dark in the water as well*). Similarly, the Theme of the third main clause, *some fishes that live in areas of the ocean where there is no light*, further develops the point presented in the Rheme of the second main clause (*varies greatly among fishes*). This way of structuring text enables the author to successively add more information about fish.

Text 9 demonstrates that Theme/Rheme structure in scientific texts often features what Eggins (2004) calls a "zig-zagging" pattern of development, meaning that the information in the Rheme of one clause appears again, often in different wording, in the Theme of the next clause. Text 10 further illustrates this pattern, as shown in Figure 2.2, a Theme/Rheme analysis of Text 10.

> Text 10: One of the places where groundwater is heated is in Yellowstone National Park in Wyoming. Yellowstone has hot springs and geysers. A geyser is a hot spring that erupts periodically, shooting water and steam into the air. Groundwater is heated to high temperatures, causing it to expand underground. This expansion forces some of the water out of the ground, taking the pressure off of the remaining water. The remaining water boils quickly, with much of it turning into steam. The steam shoots out of the opening like steam out of a teakettle, forcing the remaining water out with it. Yellowstone's famous geyser, Old Faithful, shoots between 14,000 and 32,000 L of water and steam into the air on average once every 80 minutes. (From *Science Voyages*, 2000b, p. 352)

FIGURE 2.2
The Zig-Zagging Pattern of Thematic Progression in Scientific Writing

Clause	Theme	Rheme
1.	One of the places where groundwater is heated	is in Yellowstone National Park in Wyoming.
2.	Yellowstone	has hot springs and geysers.
3.	A geyser	is a hot spring that erupts periodically,
4.	(the hot spring)	shooting water and steam into the air.
5.	Groundwater	is heated to high temperatures,
6.	(high temperatures)	causing it to expand underground.
7.	This expansion	forces some of the water out of the ground,
8.	(some of the water out)	taking the pressure off of the remaining water.
9.	The remaining water	boils quickly,
10.	with much of it	turning into steam.
11.	The steam	shoots out of the opening like steam out of a teakettle,
12.	(the steam)	forcing the remaining water out with it.
13.	Yellowstone's famous geyser, Old Faithful,	shoots between 14,000 and 32,000 L of water and steam into the air on average once every 80 minutes.

In explaining the formation of geysers, Text 10 contains a total of 13 non-embedded clauses and, thus, 13 Themes. (Themes that are not stated explicitly are shown in parentheses in Figure 2.2.) Each Theme recapitulates what has been stated in the Rheme of a previous clause, enabling the next clause to further comment on or develop that information. For example, the Theme in Clause 1, *one of the places where groundwater is heated*, rephrases what has been said in the prior text about underground water being heated by rocks that come in contact with molten material beneath Earth's surface (not excerpted here). This is further expanded upon by adding more information, a location where groundwater can be found *(in Yellowstone Park)*. Similarly, the majority of the clauses in this text recast the information presented in the Rheme of the previous clause (underlined) in their Themes and then further develop it. Note, in particular, that in Clause 7, the nominalization *This expansion* synthesizes what is said in Clause 6 into an abstract entity so that it can become the subject of the ensuing discussion. Clauses 10 and 12 each reiterate the Theme in the previous clause in order to elaborate on what *The remaining water* (Clauses 9–10) and *The steam* (Clauses 11–12) do. Clause 13, at the end of the paragraph, names one famous geyser that exemplifies the definition of geyser and the process described in the text. This pattern of Thematic progression creates a text that flows from one clause to the next, allowing the author to successively build the explanation and provide an accurate and coherent account of the formation of one type of underground hot spring called a geyser.

This kind of highly structured scientific writing may present a challenge to students who are used to the kind of discourse structuring more typical of everyday language. In everyday conversation, speakers are typically responding to each other and maintaining a focus on a particular topic, so the Themes are often pronouns referring either to the interactants themselves (*I, you*) or to the thing being talked about (*it, that*, etc.) (Eggins, 2004; Schleppegrell, 2004). In descriptive writing too, the writer can introduce a topic and then use pronouns to maintain it as Theme (Fang, 2005a). But in scientific texts, the Themes are more varied, as a writer develops an explanation, moving from Rheme to Theme with lengthy and abstract Themes (e.g., *One of the places where groundwater is heated, this expansion*). Reading text that constantly accumulates and develops information in this way can be challenging.

WORKING WITH STUDENTS

Students can find their way into the technical, abstract, dense, and tightly knit language of science through functional language analysis, where grammar is interpreted as a resource for making meaning rather than as a set of rules to be followed. Learning the technical vocabulary is an obvious challenge. Teachers can help students learn to analyze words with Greek or Latin origins by recognizing the meaning of the parts in a word (e.g., prefix, suffix, root) and then putting them together to think about the meaning of the word as a whole. For example, the word *phytoremediation*, which means the use of plants to clean up contaminated land, is made up of five meaningful parts: the prefixes *phyto* ("plant") and *re* ("back"), the root *medi* ("to heal"), and the suffixes *ate* ("to act upon in a specified manner") and *tion* ("process"). Teachers and students can also explore where words come from and how they function in the text, how some words are metaphors that carry over from one context to another, and how words have different meanings depending on the context of use.

Students can learn to handle abstract nouns through practice in unpacking scientific language. Teachers can raise students' awareness of the role nominalization plays in the development of science and cultivation of scientific thinking and reasoning, helping them recapture the actors and other information that may be lost in nominalization. For example, the information presented in Text 4 (p. 25) might be more accessibly reported as: *Einstein explained how certain metals can eject electrons when light falls on them. Eleven years later, another American physicist Robert Millikan conducted experiments to test Einstein's theory. He was able to confirm everything Einstein had said. One of the theories he confirmed was that when a light wave travels more cycles per second, each individual photon possesses a higher amount of energy.* Such a translation requires both linguistic knowledge and science content knowledge, as it involves more than a simple manipulation of linguistic structures (turning verbs and adjectives into nouns). This is why analysis and discussion of language is important: so that where the language itself does not fully represent the meaning in ways accessible to students, such as when agency is suppressed through nominalization, teachers can help unpack and supply meaning. At the same time, students can also practice using the technical and abstract language of science in hands-on activities so that they become familiar with the ways that meaning is repackaged grammatically in writing and reporting science.

Unpacking scientific language can be a regular part of science instruction through both oral and written practices. Teachers can model the deconstruction of nominalizations in science texts when reading aloud or reading with students, purposefully switching back and forth between the formal scientific expressions and more everyday wording that helps students understand the scientific concepts and principles. After reading, students can summarize or synthesize what they have read in writing that draws on more familiar language patterns. They can also rewrite some excerpts of their science texts for a younger audience, where doing so does not lose scientific meaning or content. In classes where writing is used regularly to support science learning, students can compare and contrast their own writing with text excerpts from textbooks or trade books on similar topics, focusing on how the use of nominalization, or its lack, impacts these texts' effectiveness in presenting information, developing arguments, and creating text flow.

Students can also learn to deconstruct lengthy noun groups into their parts (pre-modifier, head, post-modifier) or, conversely, to add pre- and/or post-modifiers to a head noun, creating (for example, with *disaster*) a long noun group such as *the most destructive natural disaster that has ever been recorded in the history of Louisiana*. Teachers can also have students identify noun groups of varying length and complexities in the texts they read, comparing and contrasting how nouns are used in texts written for different audiences and purposes. They can also discuss how nouns are typically expanded by identifying the specific grammatical forms (e.g., adjective, noun, prepositional phrase, embedded clause) that serve as pre- or post-modifiers. Calculating and comparing the lexical density indices of different texts can help students recognize that texts often vary in their informational loads depending on their topics, purposes, and intended audiences.

Finally, students can engage in activities that develop their awareness of the organization of scientific texts through an analysis of the Theme/Rheme structure, looking in particular at the patterns of Thematic progression. For example, they can track the Themes in a text to identify the "zig-zagging" structure or the reiterating structure—that is, patterns that hold a Theme constant (e.g., *the remaining water . . . much of it*). Teachers and students can develop a text together, with students creating a complex noun group or nominalization that synthesizes what has been said so that it can become the Theme of the next clause. This allows students to see how a large chunk of information can be repackaged for use in subsequent discussion. Comparison of textbook or trade book excerpts with students' own writing can also help them recognize how scientists structure their texts in ways that facilitate presentation of information and development of logical reasoning.

Table 2.1 summarizes the key discourse features of science, the grammatical resources that realize these features, the language analysis strategies for helping students recognize the meaning in these features, and sample classroom-based activities for engaging students in language analysis and exploration. These language-focused activities can be integrated into an inquiry-based science pedagogy to promote science literacy development for all students (Fang, Lamme, & Pringle, 2009).

Science uses language in ways that are distinct from everyday ways of using language. It draws heavily on nouns as a grammatical resource to create texts that are simultaneously technical, abstract, dense, and tightly knit. In order to make such texts accessible to students, an emphasis on technical vocabulary alone is not enough. In the construction of a scientific theory, it is the grammar, not just words alone, that

TABLE 2.1
Working with the Language of Science

Discourse Features	Grammatical Resources	Analysis Strategies	Classroom Activities
Technical	• Words that are unique to science • Everyday words with specialized meanings	Analyze technical words	• Deconstruct words to recognize prefix, suffix, and root • Recognize where words come from and how they function in the text • Discuss how words have different meanings depending on the context of use • Use new technical terms in multiple ways in science activities
Abstract	• Nominalization	Analyze abstract nouns	• Unpack nominalizations to recover agency and resolve ambiguity • Rewrite science texts for a younger audience where possible • Compare use of nominalization in science texts of different kinds
Dense	• Long, complex noun groups	Analyze lengthy noun groups	• Deconstruct noun groups • Expand simple nouns into noun groups with pre- and post-modifiers • Identify and compare noun groups of varying complexities in different texts • Calculate and compare lexical density indices in different text types and in texts written by the expert and the novice
Tightly Knit	• Lexicalized, lengthy, or abstract nouns as Themes • Zig-zagging or reiterating patterns of Thematic development	Analyze Theme-Rheme structure	• Track clause Themes • Create effective Themes in joint text construction • Compare Thematic patterns in science texts of different genres and by different writers

enables scientists to create technical meanings and a form of discourse for reasoning. Through functional language analysis, teachers can help their students recognize how these specialized patterns of language construct scientific knowledge and values. A focus on the structure and functions of nouns and noun groups, in particular, provides a window into important realms of scientific meanings and illuminates the challenges of science reading. With this focus, teachers can better develop their students' abilities "to read science, to reason with science, and to use science later in life" (Lemke, 1990, p. 172).

One of the key goals of the science education curriculum should be to support students in developing the ability to cope with the distinctive linguistic features of science so that they can more effectively access, comprehend, and produce science texts. As Wellington and Osborne (2001) have argued, "paying more attention to language is one of the most important acts that can be done to improve the quality of science education" (p. 1). It is not helpful to dismiss secondary science reading materials as simply "poorly written" or "lifeless." Instead, teachers have a responsibility to provide instruction that enhances students' capacity to understand and use the language of science. Functional language analysis enables teachers to do just that.

chapter 3

Interpretation and Reasoning in History: Beyond Text Structures

Explicit, shared knowledge about how language works in history enables teachers to focus students' attention on both form and function, and . . . this helps them to analyse critically historical discourse as well as independently construct their own meanings.

—Coffin, 2006a, p. 169

Textbooks are a major resource for secondary school history teachers. But history textbooks are densely packed with information and often lack elaboration and clear connections, making them difficult to read (Beck & McKeown, 1994; McKeown & Beck, 1994). Some teachers respond to this difficulty by asking students to read less or by summarizing information in charts or other graphic organizers for students. Such approaches, however, may only present fragments that form no coherent picture for students of what history is about and rarely lead students to interrogate the texts or analyze the interpretations the texts present. Textbooks represent choices by authors and publishers about the events and actors they highlight and foreground. Students can get access to the dense and abstract language of the textbook by analyzing the wording that constructs time and cause, attributes agency, and presents judgment and interpretation. Engaging in conversation about these issues in the classroom promotes disciplinary learning and critical literacy as students recognize how language choices contribute to the presentation of history.

History textbook chapters are typically made up of short sections that present different patterns of text that respond to different functional purposes: to chronicle or retell events, to describe, or to present explanations or debates. Text structures that teachers are typically recommended to help students recognize—such as listing, sequence, compare/contrast, cause/effect, or problem/solution (Readence, Bean, & Baldwin, 2004; Vacca & Vacca, 2005)—do not often correspond with these sections, and subheadings do not always indicate where shifts in meaning and function occur. Functional linguists have described the language features of secondary school texts that can be brought to students' attention as they read and write history (e.g., Achugar & Schleppegrell, 2005; Coffin, 2004, 2006b; Martin, 2002; Schleppegrell, 2005; Schleppegrell & Achugar, 2003; Schleppegrell, Achugar, & Oteíza, 2004; Schleppegrell & de Oliveira, 2006). A functional analysis of language can help students learn to recognize how the language changes as the text presents different perspectives on history. It enables teachers to go beyond generic text structure labels to help students see how historical meanings are constructed in recurring patterns related to the goals and purposes of history instruction.

ANALYZING HISTORY TEXTS

A passage from a tenth grade world history textbook chapter about the American Revolution (Beck, Black, Krieger, Naylor, & Shabakam, 2003, pp. 184–185) illustrates how students can focus on language patterns to better comprehend the content (**experiential meaning**), interpretation (**interpersonal meaning**), and organization (**textual meaning**) of their history texts. The passage has three sections, reproduced in Figure 3.1: Growing Hostility Leads to War, Enlightenment Ideas Influence American Colonists, and Success for the Colonists. Within the section Enlightenment Ideas Influence American Colonists is a quote from the *Declaration of Independence* under the heading A VOICE FROM THE PAST, an example of how a primary source text is often incorporated into history textbooks.

Every text has its own character. This particular text in Figure 3.1, written by experts in world history, presents one perspective on events that another history textbook might not. Functional language analysis reveals the structure, content, and perspective of this and other secondary history texts because it focuses students on motifs that are central to history—the interaction of time and cause and the foregrounding and backgrounding of interpretation. History is about what brought about or followed from events through time, and the fact that all events have

FIGURE 3.1
The Textbook Sections

Growing Hostility Leads to War   Over the next decade, further events steadily led to war. Some colonial leaders, such as Boston's Samuel Adams, favored independence from Britain. They encouraged conflict with British authorities. At the same time, George III and his ministers made enemies of many moderate colonists by their harsh stands. In 1773, to protest an import tax on tea, Adams organized a raid against three British ships in Boston Harbor. The raiders dumped 342 chests of tea into the water. George III, infuriated by the "Boston Tea Party," as it was called, ordered the British navy to close the port of Boston. British troops occupied the city.

In September 1774, representatives from every colony except Georgia gathered in Philadelphia to form the First Continental Congress. This group protested the treatment of Boston. When the king paid little attention to the complaints, all 13 colonies decided to form the Second Continental Congress to debate their next move.

On April 19, 1775, British soldiers and American militiamen exchanged gunfire on the village green in Lexington, Massachusetts. The fighting spread to nearby Concord. When news of the fighting reached the Second Continental Congress, its members voted to raise an army under the command of a Virginian named George Washington. The American Revolution had begun.

Enlightenment Ideas Influence American Colonists   Although a war had begun, the American colonists still debated their attachment to Great Britain. A growing number, however, favored independence. They heard the persuasive arguments of colonial leaders such as Patrick Henry, John Adams, and Benjamin Franklin. These leaders used Enlightenment ideas to justify independence. The colonists had asked for the same political rights as people in Britain, they said, but the king had stubbornly refused. Therefore, the colonists were justified in rebelling against a tyrant who had broken the social contract.

In July 1776, the Second Continental Congress issued the **Declaration of Independence.** This document, written by **Thomas Jefferson,** was firmly based on the ideas of John Locke and the Enlightenment. The Declaration reflected these ideas in its eloquent argument for natural rights.

A VOICE FROM THE PAST

We hold these truths to be self-evident, that all Men are created equal, that they are endowed by their Creator with certain unalienable Rights, that among these are Life, Liberty, and the

Pursuit of Happiness; that to secure these Rights, Governments are instituted among Men, deriving their just Powers from the Consent of the Governed.

—Declaration of Independence

Since Locke had asserted that people had the right to rebel against an unjust ruler, the Declaration of Independence included a long list of George III's abuses. The document ended by breaking the ties between the colonies and Britain. The colonies, the Declaration said, "are absolved from all allegiance to the British crown."

Success for the Colonists   When war was first declared, the odds seemed heavily weighted against the Americans. Washington's ragtag, poorly trained army faced the well-trained forces of the most powerful country in the world. In the end, however, the Americans won their war for independence.

Several reasons explain their success. First, the Americans' motivation for fighting was much stronger than that of the British, since their army was defending their homeland. Second, the overconfident British generals made several mistakes. Third, time itself was on the side of the Americans. The British could win battle after battle, as they did, and still lose the war. Fighting an overseas war, 3,000 miles from London, was terribly expensive. After a few years, tax-weary British citizens clamored for peace.

Finally, the Americans did not fight alone. Louis XVI of France had little sympathy for the ideals of the American Revolution, but he was eager to weaken France's rival, Britain. French entry into the war in 1778 was decisive. In 1781, combined forces of about 9,500 Americans and 7,800 French trapped a British army commanded by Lord Cornwallis near Yorktown, Virginia. Unable to escape, Cornwallis surrendered. The Americans were victorious.

multiple causes means that historians use language carefully when they are constructing explanations. Textbooks use strategies that make the interpretation more or less explicit or more or less naturalized through the narrative of events. Discussing how causes and interpretation are constructed in particular texts enables students to get more out of the history they read.

By asking and answering three questions about language, students can engage in close reading of a history text to explore its meaning. The questions are:

- How did the author organize this section?
- What is going on in the text?
- What is the perspective of the author?

Answering these questions involves moving through the text clause by clause, focusing in turn on the meaningful constituents of each clause and the textual, experiential, and interpersonal meanings they present. The first step is to identify the **Theme** of each clause. Analysis of Themes and the conjunctions that often appear in Themes helps students identify **textual meaning** in the way the text is organized according to time, cause, contrast, or condition. Then the **process types** are identified to determine which types of processes are most prominent. Analysis of clause **processes**, **participants**, and **circumstances** helps students recognize the **experiential meanings** and can stimulate discussion about how events and actors are represented. The **interpersonal meaning** in history texts is constructed in the interpretation built in by the author, and a close look at an author's choice of process types, the presentation of different kinds of participants, and the reasoning constructed in the way time and cause are presented reveals how this interpretation is constructed. The three kinds of meaning are always made simultaneously, and answering the three questions enables students to see the interplay of the language resources in the construction of historical interpretation. It also helps them recognize the language choices as options chosen to present a particular view of history, thereby also encouraging a critical reading perspective.

A CHRONICLING TEXT

The first section of the text in Figure 3.1, with the subheading Growing Hostility Leads to War, presents a sequence of events that led to the American Revolution, a chronicling pattern that is frequent in history as an author develops an account of what happened.

How Did the Author Organize This Section?

The first question to ask about a text is, *How did the author organize this section?* The kind of organization in focus is the overall pattern of meaning that the text presents, as well as the strategies used for moving from clause to clause within the text. Often the subheadings or first sentences of subsections in history textbooks summarize what will then be presented, as in the text following the subhead: *Over the next decade, further events steadily led to war.* Students can learn to recognize this pattern of generalization in a topic sentence that provides the main point that will be developed.

The key organizing resource in the language for moving from clause to clause is the Theme, the first experiential constituent (the first process, participant, or circumstance) in the clause, along with any conjunctions or prepositions that precede it. In history, many clauses begin with grammatical circumstances, realized in prepositional phrases and adverbs. Grammatical circumstances construct meaning about time, place, manner, etc. (as shown in the chart).

CIRCUMSTANTIAL MEANING	EXAMPLE (CIRCUMSTANCES UNDERLINED)
Time when, how long, how often	<u>Over the next decade,</u> events led to war.
Place where, how far, how often	They gathered <u>in Philadelphia</u>.
Manner how, with what, like what	They made enemies <u>by their harsh stands</u>.

In Figure 3.2, the clauses in this part of the whole text are numbered, with Themes in bold. The Themes that organize this section include dates and other time markers as well as the key historical actors.

Circumstances presented in prepositional phrases (Clauses 1, 4, 5, 12, and 17) are Themes that construct the time sequence in this text. Clauses 14 and 19, introduced with the word *When*, move events forward at the same time they establish the motivation for the colonists' and Congress' actions. These Themes indicate that this text is organized as a chronology, a recount of a sequence of events. Key actors in the events, the grammatical participants constructed in noun groups, also serve as Themes (e.g., Clauses 2, 7, and 15). Related Themes, such as *Some colonial leaders, such as Boston's Samuel Adams* (Clause 2), the pronoun *they* (Clause 3), the repetition of *Adams* (Clause 6), and *the raiders* (Clause 7) enable the author to present a cohesive chain of actors and activities. In Paragraph 3, the Themes of Clauses 18 and 19 reconstrue *British soldiers and American militiamen exchanged gunfire* (Clause 17) as *the fighting*. The Theme of Clause 21, *The American Revolution*, identifies all of the events in this sequence as comprising the beginning of a key moment in American his-

FIGURE 3.2
Clauses and Themes in the Chronicling Text

Growing Hostility Leads to War

(1) **Over the next decade,** further events steadily led to war. (2) **Some colonial leaders, such as Boston's Samuel Adams,** favored independence from Britain. (3) **They** encouraged conflict with British authorities. (4) **At the same time,** George III and his ministers made enemies of many moderate colonists by their harsh stands. (5) **In 1773,** to protest an import tax on tea, (6) **Adams** organized a raid against three British ships in Boston Harbor. (7) **The raiders** dumped 342 chests of tea into the water. (8) **George III,** << (9) infuriated by the "Boston Tea Party,"(10) **as it** was called,>> ordered the British navy to close the port of Boston.[1] (11) **British troops** occupied the city.

(12) **In September 1774,** representatives from every colony except Georgia gathered in Philadelphia to form the First Continental Congress. (13) **This group** protested the treatment of Boston. (14) **When the king** paid little attention to the complaints, (15) **all 13 colonies** decided to form the Second Continental Congress (16) to debate their next move.

(17) **On April 19, 1775,** British soldiers and American militiamen exchanged gunfire on the village green in Lexington, Massachusetts. (18) **The fighting** spread to nearby Concord. (19) **When news of the fighting** reached the Second Continental Congress, (20) **its members** voted to raise an army under the command of a Virginian named George Washington. (21) **The American Revolution** had begun.

tory. Students can identify these Themes to explore how the author has developed and organized the sequence of events. Using the progression of Themes to answer the question *How is this text organized?* shows that the author has linked events by using time and key historical actors as the departure points for the sequence of clauses that build to the moment when the American Revolution begins.

What Is Going On in the Text?

The second question, *What is going on in the text?* can be answered by identifying the processes presented in each clause, classifying them as

---

[1]Clause 8 is "interrupted" by two other clauses, marked in chevron brackets (<< >>). Some kinds of dependent clauses (e.g., Clause 9) cannot be analyzed for Theme. These points are explained further in Chapter 5.

doing, sensing, saying, and **being.** Each clause presents one of these four kinds of processes, indicating when an author is recounting events (**doing** processes), describing or defining (**being** processes), or telling what historical actors have said, thought, or felt (**saying** or **sensing** processes). Recognizing the process type also highlights the different roles of the grammatical participants. Grammatical participants are typically constructed in the nouns and noun groups, referring to the people, things, institutions, or entities engaged in the processes of **doing, sensing, saying,** and **being.** Analyzing the participant roles focuses attention on how the author represents historical actors, the different power relations between these actors, and whose thoughts and words are represented by the author, as well as what is being defined and described, and how.

Table 3.1 presents the different process types and participant roles. In **doing** processes, participants may be **Actors** or **Goals**; in **sensing** processes, they are **Senser** and **Phenomenon**; in **saying** processes, they are **Sayer** and **Message**; and in **being** processes they may be the **Carrier** and **Attribute** when something is described or the **Token** and **Value** when something is defined.

Classifying process type is not done just on the basis of the meaning of the verb alone; it is based on the meaning of the clause as a whole. An analysis of the processes, participants, and circumstances in this chronicling text is presented in Table 3.2. All of the processes in this text except for that in Clause 2 (italicized), which is a **sensing** process, are **doing** processes that chronicle the events that led to the American Revolution.

Constructing a chart like Table 3.2 is not just a question of copying the language from the text into boxes in a linear process. Students have to think about the meaning in each clause as they do the analysis. For example, the analysis of Clauses 8–10 comes from the sentence:

> George III, *infuriated* by the "Boston Tea Party," as it *was called*, *ordered* the British navy to close the port of Boston.

This sentence has three clauses with three processes: *infuriate, call,* and *order. Call* is a **being** process, telling us that the events that day have been named the "Boston Tea Party." Identifying the process type depends on the context and not just on the meaning of the verb in isolation. In another context, *call* might be a **saying** process ("Come here," he called). This sentence also shows us that the Actors and Goals of **doing** processes

TABLE 3.1
Processes and Participant Roles

Process Type	Participant Roles	Function	Example (Participants underlined)
Doing	Actor	the one who does the deed or performs the doing	<u>The raiders</u> destroyed the tea.
	Goal	the one or thing to whom the doing is directed	The raiders destroyed <u>the tea.</u>
Sensing	Senser	the one who thinks, feels, or perceives	<u>Some colonial leaders</u> favored independence from Britain.
	Phenomenon	that which is thought, felt, or perceived	Some colonial leaders favored <u>independence from Britain.</u>
Saying	Sayer	the one who/that says	<u>*The Declaration of Independence*</u> said, "The colonies are absolved from all allegiance to the British crown."
	Message	what is said	*The Declaration of Independence* said, <u>"The colonies are absolved from all allegiance to the British crown."</u>
Being	Carrier	the one to which/ whom a quality is ascribed	<u>Fighting an overseas war</u> was terribly expensive.
	Attribute	the quality being ascribed	Fighting an overseas war was <u>terribly expensive.</u>
	Token	that which stands for what is being defined	<u>The event</u> was called the "Boston Tea Party."
	Value	that which defines	The event was called <u>the "Boston Tea Party."</u>

TABLE 3.2
Participant/Process Analysis of **Doing** Processes in the
Chronicling Text

Clause	Circumstance/ Conjunction	Participant (Actor)	Process (Doing)	Participant (Goal)	Circumstance
1	Over the next decade,	further events	steadily led		to war.
2		*Some colonial leaders, such as Boston's Samuel Adams*	*favored*	*independence from Britain.*[1]	
3		They	encouraged	conflict with British authorities.[2]	
4	At the same time,	George III and his ministers	made	enemies of many moderate colonists	by their harsh stands.
5	In 1773,	[Adams]	to protest[3]	an import tax on tea,	
6		Adams	organized	a raid against three British ships in Boston Harbor.	
7		The raiders	dumped	342 chests of tea	into the water.
8		George III	ordered	the British navy to close the port of Boston.[4]	
9		the "Boston Tea Party," (10) <<as it was called,>> [5]	infuriated	[George III]	
11		British troops	occupied	the city.	
12	In September 1774,	representatives from every colony except Georgia	gathered to form	the First Continental Congress.	in Philadelphia
13		This group	protested	the treatment of Boston.	
14	When	the king	paid little attention to[6]	the complaints,	
15		all 13 colonies	decided to form	the Second Continental Congress	

16		[the Second Continental Congress]	to debate	their next move.	
17	On April 19, 1775,	British soldiers and American militiamen	exchanged	gunfire	on the village green in Lexington, Massachusetts.
18		The fighting	spread		to nearby Concord.
19	When	news of the fighting	reached	the Second Continental Congress,	
20		its members	voted to raise	an army under the command of a Virginian named George Washington.	
21		The American Revolution	had begun.		

[1] This is a **sensing** process, expressing the mental state of the colonial leaders; what they *wanted*. It is italicized to indicate that the participants are Senser and Phenomenon, not Actor and Goal.

[2] *with British authorities* is a circumstance that further defines the *conflict*. When a circumstance defines or describes a participant, we analyze it as part of that noun group.

[3] *To protest an import tax on tea* has no expressed Actor, but we can recover the Actor from the following clause. Note that *to* can be either a preposition (when followed by a noun) or part of a process (when followed by a verb).

[4] *to close* is also a process, with the British navy as Actor. Here it is presented as part of the Goal of George III's *order*; alternatively, it could also be analyzed as a separate process.

[5] *as it was called* is a **being** process, defining the Boston Tea Party.

[6] The processes *paid little attention to* and *decided to form* (Clause 15) are categorized here as **doing** rather than **sensing** because they stand for actions (or lack of them). That is, by *paying little attention*, the king *did nothing*, and the colonies, in *deciding to form* the Congress, actually formed it. Where such processes come in a sequence of actions, as here, they are best categorized as **doing** processes. Discussion about such processes and the potential to classify them in different ways helps students explore the meaning of the text.

are not always given in that order, with the Actor preceding the Goal. In this sentence *George III* is the Actor in the *order* process, but is the Goal in the *infuriate* process, where *the Boston Tea Party* is the Actor that *infuriates*. This shows why the functional, meaning-based grammar is useful for talking about a text, as structural categories such as subject and object do not bring out the meaning (*George III* is the subject of both *infuriate* and *order*). As students talk about the meaning of the processes and associated participant roles, they are learning both about history and about how language works.

Analyzing clauses in this way also calls for interpretation of clauses that do not have expressed Actors, such as *to protest an import tax on tea*

(Clause 5). Students have to infer that *Adams* (or perhaps the *raiders*) were protesting the tax, reading ahead to Clause 6, *Adams organized a raid*. In Clauses 15–16, *all 13 colonies decided to form the Second Continental Congress to debate their next move*, it is ambiguous whether the two processes, *decided to form* and *to debate* have different Actors. Table 3.2 represents the *13 colonies* as forming the Congress, and the Congress as debating the next move, but of course it is representatives of the 13 colonies that formed the Congress, so the two processes can also be understood as having the same Actor, *all 13 colonies*. Discussion about the different ways events like this are represented helps students see how the English language works, giving them a perspective they can use in reading other texts.

Students can analyze how their texts represent key historical actors and their goals, whether as concrete individuals or groups or as abstract entities (places, things, or ideas). When authors are attributing historical agency to abstractions, they can explore who the historical actors behind those abstractions might be. In this case, individuals (*Samuel Adams* in Clauses 2 and 6, *George III* in Clauses 4 and 8) and groups (e.g., *colonial leaders* in Clause 2, *British troops* in Clause 11, *representatives* in Clause 12, etc.) are named, but abstractions such as *the fighting* and *news of the fighting* (Clauses 18 and 19) are also grammatical Actors. Discussing the way the text represents these historical actors in grammatical Actors can stimulate interesting conversation about how authors present historical agency.

A focus on the Goals revealed through an analysis like that in Table 3.2 can help students recognize the sequence of events that led to the American Revolution: *conflict with British authorities, import tax on tea, raid against three British ships in Boston Harbor, 342 chests of tea, British navy to close the port of Boston*, etc. The circumstances in the clause Rhemes also contribute important meanings, constructing place (Clause 7, *into the water*, and Clause 17, *on the village green in Lexington*) and manner (Clause 4, the British made enemies *by their harsh stands*). Analyzing the meanings contributed by the processes, participants, and circumstances helps students think more deeply about what the text is about.

What Is the Perspective of the Author?

The third question to ask about a text is, *What is the perspective of the author?* Teachers already commonly look at how an author flavors a text by the choice of words. Here noun groups like the *moderate colonists* and *harsh stands* in Clause 4 color the text with meanings that position historical actors in particular ways. Another aspect of interpretation is constructed by who or what is presented as having the power to influence events. Adams and George III are both presented as powerful historical actors, as Adams *encouraged conflict* and *organized a raid*, and *George III ordered the navy to close the port*. Part of the judgment and interpretation of historians is constructed in whom they represent as having power to influence others' actions. Recognizing how time and cause interact also helps students analyze the perspective of the text. For example, the process *steadily led* in the sentence *Over the next decade, further events steadily led to war* (Clause 1) puts time and cause together, with the abstract participant *events* as the grammatical Actor: *Events* led to war. Attributing responsibility to abstractions like *events* allows the author to suggest the inevitability of the war.

These language choices show how the author is concerned with developing a sequence of events across a time span but is also building an interpretation that presents different actors in different lights. Seeing how the actors and their actions are represented helps students understand the text and see how the author's choice of words involves interpretation and judgments in the way events and actors are portrayed. Moving through a text like this, sentence by sentence and clause by clause, talking about the language choices the author has made, teachers and students can engage in rich conversation about the meaning of the passage that can help students recognize similar chronicling patterns in other texts they read.

A POINT OF VIEW TEXT

The purpose of the second section of this text, headed Enlightenment Ideas Influence American Colonists, is to show how the ideas of John Locke and the Enlightenment inspired the colonists to feel justified in declaring independence. History textbooks often interrupt the chronological retelling of events to discuss historical influences or to present different sides of an issue or debate. This type of text, in contrast to the chronicling text, is not constructed as a series of actions; rather, it presents the views of those who wanted independence from Britain and relates those to the views of the Enlightenment philosophers who inspired them. Presenting a contrast in views or a discussion about influences does not involve laying out a set of events that occurred over time, and so it calls for significantly different language resources than those used to chronicle events. The language choices shift in several ways that can be investigated by asking the same three questions we asked about the chronicling text.

How Did the Author Organize This Section?

Here again the subheading provides the preview of what is to come, helping us understand that this text lays out what those Enlightenment ideas are. The goal of the author is to help the reader understand the ideas and arguments made by the colonists. This section of the text also includes a primary source, a quotation from the *Declaration of Independence*, set off from the rest of the text in a different font.

The clauses in this section are numbered and the Themes are presented in bold in Figure 3.3 to reveal more clearly how this text is organized. Rather than construing time, the Themes in this "point of view" text mainly name the historical actors, developing a chain of reference that introduces the *American colonists* (Clause 2) and then refers to them as *A growing number* that *favored independence* (Clause 3). The colonists' views are clearly the prominent ones here. *The king* (Clause 9) appears only once as Theme, preceded by the conjunction *but* that introduces his contrasting view. Only one Theme constructs time reference, the *In July 1776* of Clause 11 that establishes the moment in time when the *Declaration of Independence* was adopted. This text also has conjunctions that function as part of the Themes in Clauses 1, 9, 10, and 22, but they are not the conjunction *when*, which helps structure the chronicling text. The conjunctions *although, but, therefore,* and *since* construct contrast and cause, indicating that points are being conceded and contrasted and that some conclusions are drawn explicitly.

The Themes in the rest of this text keep the focus on the *Declaration of Independence*. Within the primary source, the Themes help create a cohesive text. Students can recognize how the *truths* (Clause 15) are presented in Clauses 16 and 17, and that the Theme *that among these* (Clause 18) refers to the *rights* introduced in the Rheme of Clause 17.

What Is Going On in the Text?

Again, analyzing the configurations of processes, participants, and circumstances reveals *what is going on* in the text. This text uses a variety of process types, the majority of which are processes of **sensing** or **saying,** constructing the points of view of the colonists. Several are **being** processes that construct the Enlightenment philosophy and the tenets of the *Declaration of Independence*. With a text that has different process types interacting, instead of presenting the analysis of the whole text in one table, it is more useful to analyze the different process types separately to recognize the different meanings that the processes construct.

FIGURE 3.3
Clauses and Themes in the Point of View Text

Enlightenment Ideas Influence American Colonists

(1) **Although a war** had begun, (2) **the American colonists** still debated their attachment to Great Britain. (3) **A growing number**, however, favored independence. (4) **They** heard the persuasive arguments of colonial leaders such as Patrick Henry, John Adams, and Benjamin Franklin. (5) **These leaders** used Enlightenment ideas (6) to justify independence. (7) **The colonists** had asked for the same political rights as people in Britain, (8) **they** said, (9) **but the king** had stubbornly refused. (10) **Therefore, the colonists** were justified in rebelling against a tyrant who had broken the social contract.

(11) **In July 1776**, the Second Continental Congress issued the *Declaration of Independence*. (12) **This document, written by Thomas Jefferson,** was firmly based on the ideas of John Locke and the Enlightenment. (13) **The Declaration** reflected these ideas in its eloquent argument for natural rights.

A VOICE FROM THE PAST

(14) **We** hold (15) **these truths** to be self-evident, (16) **that all Men** are created equal, (17) **that they** are endowed by their Creator with certain unalienable Rights, (18) **that among these** are Life, Liberty, and the Pursuit of Happiness; (19) **that** to secure these Rights, (20) **Governments** are instituted among Men, (21) deriving their just Powers from the Consent of the Governed.
—Declaration of Independence

(22) **Since Locke** had asserted (23) **that people** had the right to rebel against an unjust ruler, (24) **the Declaration of Independence** included a long list of George III's abuses. (25) **The document** ended by breaking the ties between the colonies and Britain. (26) **The colonies**, <<(27) **the Declaration** said,>> "are absolved from all allegiance to the British crown."

The key grammatical participants in **saying** and **sensing** processes are Sayers and Sensers and the Messages or Phenomena they project or perceive (their sayings or thoughts and feelings). In analyzing the Messages and Phenomena projected by **saying** and **sensing** processes, students can identify whose views are being presented and what those views are. This helps them recognize the historical actors whose perspectives are highlighted, comparing the points of view and evaluating them. Table 3.3 shows the different Sayers and Sensers and what they think or feel (the Messages or Phenomena) in this passage.

There are four different Sayers/Sensers represented here: the colonists, the king, Locke, and the *Declaration of Independence*. Documents, laws, rulings, etc., are often represented by historians as having power to speak, so it is important for students to become aware of this strategy. Representing the colonists as having the same point of view as Locke and *the Declaration* adds weight or credibility to their position.

Messages and Phenomena are often complex noun groups or clauses that can also be analyzed for their meanings. For example, in Clause 4, *the persuasive arguments of colonial leaders such as Patrick Henry, John Adams, and Benjamin Franklin* can be unpacked as *Patrick Henry, John Adams, and Benjamin Franklin argued persuasively*. Discussion of the Messages also enables discussion about how the Enlightenment philosophy contributed ideas to the *Declaration of Independence*.

The features of the Enlightenment philosophy become clearer through analysis of the other major process type in this text, the **being** process (see Table 3.4). **Being** processes in verbs like *be, have, seem,* and *become*

TABLE 3.3
Sayers/Thinkers and Their Messages/Phenomena
in the Point of View Text

Clause	Sayer/Senser	Process	Message/Phenomenon
2	American colonists	still debated	their attachment to Great Britain.
3	A growing number (of American colonists)	favored	independence.
4	They	heard	the persuasive arguments of colonial leaders such as Patrick Henry, John Adams, and Benjamin Franklin.
7	The colonists	had asked for	the same political rights as people in Britain
9	the king	had stubbornly refused.	
22	Locke	had asserted	that people had the right to rebel against an unjust ruler
27	the Declaration	said,	"The colonies are absolved from all allegiance to the British crown."

TABLE 3.4
Being Processes in the Point of View Text

Clause	Carrier	Process	Attribute
10	the colonists	were	justified in rebelling against a tyrant who had broken the social contract.[1]
12	This document, written by Thomas Jefferson,	was	firmly based on the ideas of John Locke and the Enlightenment.
13	The Declaration	reflected	these ideas in its eloquent argument for natural rights.
24	the Declaration of Independence	included	a long list of George III's abuses.

[1]Clauses 10 and 12 are analyzed as **being** processes because Clause 10 is analogous to saying the colonists were *confident;* and Clause 12 is analogous to saying the document *has* the ideas of Locke and the Enlightenment.

construct what the *Declaration of Independence* says and relate it to the Enlightenment philosophy. Students can discuss what is being defined and described here as the author presents judgments about the colonists' actions and tells what the *Declaration of Independence* includes.

There are also some **doing** processes in this text, as shown in Table 3.5. In the first **doing** process (Clause 5), the leaders are *using* Enlightenment ideas, but it is the *ideas* that justify independence in Clause 6; this is an important point that helps construct the author's perspective. Clause 25 tells us that the *document* broke the ties between the colonies and Britain, attributing agency to the document itself in a phrase that tells us how the document ended. In Clause 26, the first participant in the

TABLE 3.5
Doing Processes in the Point of View Text

Clause	Actor	Process	Goal
5	These leaders	used	Enlightenment ideas
6	[Enlightenment ideas]	to justify	independence.
11	the Second Continental Congress	issued	the Declaration of Independence.
25	The document	ended by breaking ("broke")	the ties between the colonies and Britain.
26	[???]	absolved from all allegiance to the British crown	the colonies

clause, *the colonies*, is the Goal of the action *absolving*, and not the Actor, even though it comes first in the clause. The sentence, *The colonies, the Declaration said, "are absolved from all allegiance to the British crown,"* has two clauses—Clause 27, with the **saying** process that projects what the *Declaration* said, and Clause 26, the Message projected by the **saying** process: *The colonies are absolved from all allegiance to the British crown.* The Actor in the **doing** process *(are absolved)* within this Message is not identified, as passive voice allows the author to present this process without an Actor. Students can discuss who or what absolved the colonies from allegiance to Britain; that will lead them to think about the role of documents and declarations in making things happen politically. The meaning of difficult sentences like this can be clarified through analysis and discussion; the meaning of *British Crown* as a metaphor for England may also need to be a focus. Such discussion can help students read similar passages independently with greater understanding.

The *Declaration* itself is a primary source, and reading primary sources is especially challenging because of their often formal and archaic language. Table 3.6 shows that the passage quoted from the *Declaration* is made up mainly of **doing** and **being** processes (in bold) that are projected as what the writers *hold* (meaning "believe").

The **being** clauses establish that men are equal and define the *rights;* the **doing** processes establish that these rights have been given to *Men, by their Creator,* that the purpose of governments is to secure the rights, and that governments get their power from the governed. The **doing**

TABLE 3.6
Process Types in a Primary Source Document: *Declaration of Independence*

Clause	Text	Process Type
14	We **hold**	sensing
15	these truths to **be** (are) self-evident,	being
16	that all Men **are created** equal,	being
17	that they **are endowed** by their Creator with certain unalienable Rights,	doing
18	that among these **are** Life, Liberty, and the Pursuit of Happiness;	being
19	that << **to secure** these Rights,>>	doing
20	<< >> Governments **are instituted** among Men	doing
21	**deriving** their just Powers from the Consent of the Governed.	doing

is constructed in clauses in which the Actors are either not given or are represented obliquely (*by their Creator; from the Consent of the Governed*). Taking the time to analyze and discuss the meanings in these clauses to show how they have been constructed can enhance students' understanding of the text.

This point of view text, then, has a lot going on in it: **saying, doing, and being.** It is organized to present the Enlightenment philosophy that inspired the *Declaration of Independence*, constructing the thinking and saying of those who were influenced by this philosophy and defining what it promotes. By looking in turn at each of these process types and the meanings they contribute, students can recognize the main notions that the author is presenting and see whose points of view are presented, analyze the content of the points of view, and recognize what is being defined and described.

What Is the Perspective of the Author?

Having analyzed the organization and what the text is about, students can answer the third question, *What is the perspective of the author?* through a focus on historical agency, on whose words and ideas are represented, and on how time and cause are constructed. Here the author represents the *ideas* and *document* as powerful and agentive. The **saying/sensing** processes and the Messages/Phenomena they project (Table 3.3) show the colonists, Locke, and the *Declaration* as the most prominent voices, with the king's role only that of "refusing." King George is characterized as *stubborn* and *unjust.* The *Declaration* is characterized as having an *eloquent argument for natural rights,* and word choices like *the persuasive argument* and *Enlightenment ideas justify independence* present an interpretation and point of view. The point is made explicit in the *Therefore* that introduces *the colonists were justified in rebelling against a tyrant who had broken the social contract,* where the causal conjunction highlights the key point. Analysis of these language features can help students recognize what they are being positioned by the author to believe.

This point of view text section, rather than constructing a chronicle of events, instead pauses, in a sense, to build up some background understanding about the motivations of the colonists. The text relies mainly on **saying** and **sensing** processes to present the views of those who wrote the *Declaration of Independence* and the philosophers who inspired them. It also uses **being** processes to make judgments about their actions and to lay out the key provisions of the *Declaration*. And instead of constructing causal reasoning through a naturalized conflation of time and cause, as in the chronicling text, this section is explicit in saying the colonists had not only a right but also a responsibility to rebel against a tyrant.

AN EXPLANATION TEXT

The third section, Success for the Colonists, constructs yet another pattern common in history textbooks. Rather than presenting an account of events or a contrast between different points of view, this text explicitly presents an explanation. The three questions again help investigate the meaning in the text.

How Did the Author Organize This Section?

We can again see how the text is organized by looking at how it begins and at the clause Themes. Figure 3.4 presents the clauses (numbered) in this explanation, with the Themes in bold.

The subheading gives the overall point. The text's first short paragraph sets up the challenge for the Americans before moving on to the reasons for their success, using the conjunction *however* (Clause 4) to juxtapose the heavily weighted odds against the Americans and the fact that they won in spite of those odds. Other contrastive conjunctions (*but, whereas,* etc.) are also often used in history textbooks to construct contrasts and counter expectations, and students can become aware of the meanings they present.

The organization of this text as an explanation is introduced in the first sentence of the second paragraph, *Several reasons explain their success* (Clause 5). At first glance, the Themes in Clauses 6–15 might seem to be constructing passage through time: *First, Second, Third, After a few years,* and *Finally.* But on closer inspection, we see that in fact, the *First, Second, Third,* and *Finally* construct a rhetorical organization that presents a series of reasons, enabling the author to introduce the *several reasons* one by one. What seem to be markers of chronology are not introducing events that happened in a particular order but are instead the set of explanatory points that the author has constructed and ordered to make the argument about why the colonists won. This is the type of thesis-driven text that teachers often want their students to write, and students can be made aware of these conjunctions as resources they might adopt in their own writing. The Themes in this section, then, indicate that an explanation is being constructed, with reasons that explain the success of the American Revolution.

FIGURE 3.4
Clauses and Themes in the Explanation Text

Success for the Colonists

(1) **When war** was first declared, (2) **the odds** seemed heavily weighted against the Americans. (3) **Washington's ragtag, poorly trained army** faced the well-trained forces of the most powerful country in the world. (4) **In the end,** however, the Americans won their war for independence.

(5) **Several reasons** explain their success. (6) **First, the Americans' motivation for fighting** was much stronger than that of the British, (7) **since their army** was defending their homeland. (8) **Second, the overconfident British generals** made several mistakes. (9) **Third, time itself** was on the side of the Americans. (10) **The British** could win battle after battle, (11) **as they** did, (12) and still lose the war. (13) **Fighting an overseas war,** 3,000 miles from London, was terribly expensive. (14) **After a few years**, tax-weary British citizens clamored for peace.

(15) **Finally, the Americans** did not fight alone. (16) **Louis XVI of France** had little sympathy for the ideals of the American Revolution, (17) **but he** was eager to weaken France's rival, Britain. (18) **French entry into the war in 1778** was decisive. (19) **In 1781**, combined forces of about 9,500 Americans and 7,800 French trapped a British army commanded by Lord Cornwallis near Yorktown, Virginia. (20) **Unable to escape,** Cornwallis surrendered. (21) **The Americans** were victorious.

What Is Going On in the Text?

The question, *What is going on in the text?* can again be answered by analyzing the configurations of participants, processes, and circumstances, looking for the process types that are prominent. In this section **being** processes figure prominently, with **doing** processes interspersed. The **being** processes construct the claims of the author in general statements that evaluate, while the **doing** processes provide specific support for the claims. This is shown in Table 3.7.

In the clauses with **being** processes, students can identify what is being described (the Carrier) and how it is described (the Attribute). The grammatical participants that present the Carriers are mainly linguistic abstractions. The first reason given for the colonists' victory (Clause 6), for example, is constructed in a **nominalization**, *the Americans' motivation for fighting,* that is characterized as *much stronger than that of the British.* Other abstractions are also presented as Carriers of the Attributes that

TABLE 3.7
Being and **Doing** Processes in the Explanation Text

Clause	Participant	Process Type	Participant/Attribute
6	the Americans' motivation for fighting	was	much stronger than that of the British,
	Carrier	*Being* **Process**	**Attribute**
7	their army	was defending	their homeland.
	Actor	*Doing* **Process**	**Goal**
8	the overconfident British generals	made	several mistakes.
	Actor	*Doing* **Process**	**Goal**
9	time itself	was	on the side of the Americans.
	Carrier	*Being* **Process**	**Attribute**
10	The British	could win	battle after battle,
	Actor	*Doing* **Process**	**Goal**
11	they	did,	
	Actor	*Doing* **Process**	
12	[they]	still lose	the war.
	Actor	*Doing* **Process**	**Goal**
13	Fighting an overseas war, 3,000 miles from London,	was	terribly expensive.
	Carrier	*Being* **Process**	**Attribute**
14	tax-weary British citizens	clamored for	peace.
	Actor	*Doing* **Process**	**Goal**
15	the Americans	did not fight alone.	
	Actor	*Doing* **Process**	
18	French entry into the war in 1778	was	decisive.
	Carrier	*Being* **Process**	**Attribute**

construct reasons for the victory: *time itself was on their side* (Clause 9), and *French entry into the war* was *decisive* (Clause 18). Use of nominalization is key in constructing explanations because it enables information to be presented in a **being** process that makes a generalization or judgment (see Chapter 2 for more on nominalization). For example, processes like *motivate* and *enter* are presented as *motivation* (Clause 6) and *entry*

(Clause 18) so that they can be judged and evaluated as *much stronger* (Clause 6) and *decisive* (Clause 18).

Each generalization or judgment is then supported with information about concrete events, presented in **doing** processes. The actions provide motivation for or support of the generalization or judgment. For example, the strength of the Americans' motivation for fighting is supported by saying they were defending their homeland (Clause 7) and that the British generals made mistakes (Clause 8). The assertion that the war was expensive for Britain is supported by saying that *tax-weary British citizens clamored for peace* (Clause 14). Students can learn to recognize this pattern of generalization or judgment through **being** processes, followed by support through **doing** processes, and they can also see this as a model for their own essay writing.

What Is the Perspective of the Author?

The question, *What is the perspective of the author?* can be answered by recognizing the explicit interpretation in the presentation of reasons for the American victory in a set of causes and effects. This contrasts with the construction of cause and effect as related to the agency of the historical actors, as in the chronicling text, and with the validation of particular perspectives in the point of view text.

To present an explicit explanation about why the American Revolution was successful, the historian has shifted into more abstract language choices, where the grammatical participants are not the individuals whose words and actions we read about in the first two sections, but instead the abstractions and generalizations that enable a theory about what happened to be developed. Students can learn to recognize these patterns of evolving meaning in a text.

Working with Students

Understanding the role of language in the construction of meaning gives students insights into the strategies the author uses to construct historical events and interpretation. Table 3.8 shows how the three questions relate to the language resources that students can analyze to answer them.

As students analyze the Themes and look at the process types, they read closely, focusing on meaning. Doing this with sections of a history textbook reveals the different linguistic patterns that historians use. Students can explore whether a section is mainly about what happened by investigating whether **doing** processes, individual or collective par-

TABLE 3.8
Language Resources and Grammatical Meanings

Question	Analysis	Ask Yourself
How did the author organize this section?	Look at the macro-organization	Does the section begin with a topic sentence or short summary of what is going to be presented in the section?
	Analyze the Themes	What patterns of meaning are developed? Is the passage organized according to time? To provide comparison? To explain?
What is going on in the text?	Analyze the configurations of processes, participants, and circumstances	What process types are most frequent? What kind of participants do we find? Are participants specific or abstract? What roles do the participants play? What kinds of meanings are added in the circumstances?
What is the perspective of the author?	Analyze **doing** processes	Who is represented as agentive?
	Analyze **sensing** and **saying** processes	Whose ideas and words are represented? What do they think, feel, and say?
	Analyze **being** processes	What is defined and described? What does the author evaluate positively? Negatively?
	Analyze the causal reasoning constructed in the circumstances, conjunctions, and processes	How are time and cause constructed? What conclusions are drawn?

ticipants, and conjunctions of time and place are prominent. They can investigate whether a section is mainly about the ideas and controversies of the time by looking at the prominence of **saying** or **sensing** processes. In those processes, they can examine the Sayers and Thinkers, whether they are individuals, groups, or documents and laws. They can also examine the conjunctions of contrast and concession that enable juxtaposition of points of view. They can investigate whether a section is mainly explaining or arguing for a particular interpretation by looking for language resources that enable a rhetorical organization of point-by-point reasons, such as **being** processes, abstract participants (often constructed in nominalizations), and conjunctions of cause.

Of course, the three text patterns presented in this chapter (chronology, point of view, explanation) do not exhaust the possibilities. Sometimes authors present a situation "as it is," constructing a historical description that draws on language patterns that do not depend on time sequence. In other textbook sections, patterns of recount or biography might be found (see Coffin, 2006a, for a description of a range of genres in history textbooks). Through functional language analysis, teachers and students can develop their own taxonomies of the text patterns they find, describing the grammatical features that work together to meet the various purposes authors have in writing history.

Functional language analysis enables teachers to go beyond generic taxonomies of text structures to help students identify language patterns specific to history. Teachers report that they have been able to engage in rich discussion about history with their students by analyzing textbook sections in this way (Schleppegrell & de Oliveira, 2006), as the language analysis provides insights into how authors present history. Functional language analysis enables students to read in more than just a superficial way, interacting with and better understanding and discussing the complexities of the texts they read. Explicit discussion about the language resources that construct historical reasoning helps students better understand what they are learning, providing opportunities to create the "mindfulness" (Leinhardt, Stainton, Virji, & Odoroff, 1994) that is a key goal of history teaching. Recognizing how authors use language as a resource can help students engage with the author's interpretation, generating classroom discussions that help students construct more complex understandings.

chapter 4

Comprehending and Solving Word Problems in Mathematics: Beyond Key Words

JINGZI HUANG AND BRUCE NORMANDIA

> Too much opportunity for gaining mathematical understanding and intuition, too much practice at learning how to use mathematical meaning in real situations, is lost if mathematics is not taught, particularly at the introductory level, as a co-equal partner with language and visual representation.
>
> —Lemke, 2003, p. 231

Reading and solving word problems in mathematics involves both understanding language and applying relevant mathematical knowledge. Students who otherwise do well in mathematics often perform poorly on word problems (Wyndhamn & Säljö, 1997). For example, Kintsch (1987) found that "students do anywhere from 10–30 percent worse on word problems than when the same problem is presented in mathematical form" (p. 197). For English language learners, the difficulty is even more pronounced (Lager, 2006). One reason for this is that many students are unfamiliar with the way word problems are presented linguistically (Abedi & Lord, 2001; Kintsch, 1987; Søvik, Frostrad, & Heggberget, 1999). Mathematics teachers have tried to address this issue by adopting the "key words" approach. In this approach, teachers highlight and discuss key mathematical words (e.g., *left* suggests subtraction, *in all* suggests addition, *share* suggests division), hoping that recognizing the key words in a problem will enable students to select a mathematical operation appropriate for solving the problem. But many word problems in mathematics do not have key words (Van de Walle, 2004), and the "key words" approach does not help students understand the situation that the word problem presents (Zambo, 1994). If teachers try to simplify the very complex process of problem solving by asking students to focus on "key words" in isolation, they can lead students to ignore the meaning and structure of the problem and to fail in developing mathematical reasoning skills.

Consider this problem from elementary algebra:

Mr. Smith teaches a karate class every Monday at 4:00 PM. Initially, 26 students registered for his class. Last week 2 students withdrew from the class on Monday, 4 students withdrew from the class on Tuesday, and 3 new students registered for the class on Friday. What is the total number of students Mr. Smith currently has registered for his class?

In this example, both addition and subtraction are needed in order to solve the problem. If students focus on the key word *total*, ignoring the problem's context, they will not get a correct answer by applying only the operation of addition. Thus, as Clement and Bernhard (2005) have warned, the "key words" approach can "subvert mathematical understanding, lead to incorrect solutions, focus students' attention on values rather than quantities, and direct students toward automatically performing procedures rather than first making sense of the situation" (p. 360).

Functional language analysis is an alternative to the "key words" approach that helps students use all of the language of a word problem to identify the mathematical concepts, procedures, and principles needed to solve it. Examples from algebra and geometry textbooks for secondary students demonstrate how attention to the language patterns in word problems enables students to recognize the task that the word problem is asking them to perform, identify key information that the problem provides, and then link that information with the mathematical content they have learned so they can solve the problem.

A Guide for Solving Word Problems

Word problems in school mathematics are presented either in language alone or as a multisemiotic configuration involving language, mathematics symbolism, and visual display. In solving word problems, students first need to identify what they are being asked to do and locate relevant information in the problem. Thus, linguistic knowledge plays an important role in the initial comprehension of a word problem, initiating the building of a "situation model" relevant to the problem (Kintsch, 2004). Then, to actually solve the problem, students need to use the information presented in the problem to identify the concepts involved, the mathematical meanings to be visually represented, the mathematical symbols and formulas to be used, and the mathematical principles and procedures to be followed. Key to comprehending the text is recognizing the specialized ways mathematical concepts are constructed in language.

A set of seven questions is proposed to guide students when working through word problems. These questions are derived from the Framework of Knowledge Structures (Mohan, 1986), a heuristic informed by the work of anthropology and systemic functional linguistics for the analysis of discourse and social practice. This framework shows how any human activity, such as problem solving in mathematics, can be divided into six basic knowledge structures: **classification, description, principles, sequence, evaluation,** and **choice.** To understand and solve a problem, students need to identify the kind of problem presented **(classification)**, recognize the specific features of the problem **(description)**, know the **principles** to draw on to solve the problem and the **sequence** to follow, and then **evaluate** options for methods and solutions in order to **choose** the correct answer(s). Using these seven questions, teachers can help students find the connection between the language used in a word problem and the mathematical knowledge to be applied in solving it.

1. What is the problem to be solved?
2. What relevant information is provided in the text?
3. Which mathematical concepts are indicated or signaled in the information?
4. What are the mathematical principles needed for solving the given problem?
5. What procedures do I follow to use those principles in solving the problem?

6. As a result of these procedures, what is the solution?

7. How can I justify the solution? (Does the solution make sense?)

To answer Questions 1 and 2, students need to be able to read and comprehend the language of the word problem. Answering Questions 3–6 depends on students' knowledge of mathematics, but whether students are able to activate the mathematical schema relevant to the problem depends on understanding the language. To answer Question 7, students need to bring together the information provided in the problem and the mathematical schema they have activated.

An algebra problem for Grades 8–10 from *Algebra 1* (Larson, Boswell, Kanold, & Stiff, 2001, p. 398) and a geometry problem for Grades 9–11 from *Discovering Geometry* (Serra, 1993, p. 683) illustrate the process of using these seven questions as a guide to problem solving and demonstrate how students can use functional language analysis to comprehend and solve word problems in mathematics.

Solving a Word Problem in Algebra

> In one day the National Civil Rights Museum in Memphis, Tennessee, admitted 321 adults and children and collected $1,590. The price of admission is $6 for an adult and $4 for a child. How many adults and how many children were admitted to the museum on that day? (From *Algebra 1*, Larson, Boswell, Kanold, & Stiff, 2001, p. 398)

QUESTION 1: WHAT IS THE PROBLEM TO BE SOLVED?

To solve a word problem, students first need to identify what they are being asked to do. A problem may be asking them to solve for information or it may be directing them to act in some other ways. Teachers can help students recognize the language that specifies the task to be performed by exploring the system of **mood** in English (see Chapter 5 for more on mood). The mood system allows us to make statements **(declarative mood)**, ask questions **(interrogative mood)**, or issue commands **(imperative mood)**. There are two kinds of questions—those that request information and those that can be answered with yes or no. In mathematics word problems, questions that request information are typically constructed with expressions like *how many*, suggesting that the answer will involve a quantity; *what* or *which*, suggesting that a choice is to be made between two or more possible answers; or *why*, suggesting that a rationale is to be articulated. Questions asked with these *wh-* words can be quite complex (e.g., *In which of the following . . .?*), and practice identifying these forms can help students recognize what a problem is asking for. Questions that require yes or no responses may begin with a form of *do (does, did)* or *be (are, is, was, were)* or with a **modal verb** *(can, would, should, could,* etc.). Although students can learn to recognize the language of questions and the types of answers they call for, not all word problems ask questions. Sometimes, problems use commands *(solve, consider,* etc.) that explicitly direct students to do something to solve the problem.

In this algebra problem, the last sentence, *How many adults and how many children were admitted to the museum on that day?* asks a *wh-* question that seeks information about quantity. In addition to identifying the question, students also need to recognize that the conjunction *and* indicates that this is a two-part question, with two quantities to be determined. So recognizing mood (question or command) and the meaning in conjunctions is important for answering the question, *What is the problem to be solved?*

QUESTION 2: WHAT RELEVANT INFORMATION IS PROVIDED IN THE TEXT?

After identifying the task to be performed, students need to recognize key information provided in the problem. Analyzing **clauses** into their constituent **participants** or **attributes**, **processes**, and **circumstances** helps identify key information. Processes are constructed in verb groups that tell us what is going on in the clause; participants are constructed in noun groups that tell us *who* or *what*; attributes are constructed in adjectives in **being** processes; and circumstances are constructed in phrases that tell us *when, where, how, why,* etc. (see Chapter 3 for more on this). Students can analyze the participants, attributes, processes, and circumstances to recognize the problem situation represented in the text and identify the key entities at stake in solving the problem.

From Question 1, we know that this problem asks for information about quantities. Analyzing participants in the clauses helps us find terms that indicate quantity. The chart shows that clause participants involving quantity in this problem are: 321 adults and children (Clause 1), $1,590 (Clause 2), $6 for an adult and $4 for a child (Clause 3), and the to-be-determined number of adults and the to-be-determined number of children (Clause 4).

CLAUSES	INFORMATION PROVIDED
1. *In one day the National Civil Rights Museum in Memphis, Tennessee, admitted 321 adults and children*	**Circumstance:** *in one day* **Participant:** *the National Civil Rights Museum* **Process:** *admitted* **Participant:** *321 adults and children*
2. *and (the National Civil Rights Museum) collected $1,590.*	**Participant:** *(the National Civil Rights Museum)* **Process:** *collected* **Participant:** *$1,590*
3. *The price of admission is $6 for an adult and $4 for a child.*	**Participant:** *the price of admission* **Process:** *is* **Participant:** *$6 for an adult; $4 for a child*
4. *How many adults and how many children were admitted to the museum on that day?*	**Participant:** *unknown number of adults; unknown number of children* **Process:** *were admitted* **Circumstance:** *into the museum on that day*

Deconstructing clauses into their participants, processes, and circumstances highlights some linguistic challenges. One challenge is the **ellipsis**, the words left out or not repeated. The sentence *In one day the National Civil Rights Museum in Memphis, Tennessee, admitted 321 adults and children and collected $1,590* includes two processes, the process of *admitting* and the process of *collecting*. Students need to recognize these as separate processes with the museum as the grammatical **Actor** in both; the conjunction *and* that precedes *collected* adds a new clause. On the other hand, the *and* that links *321 adults and children* constructs one entity, the total number of people admitted. Teachers can help students recognize when a conjunction is functioning to link two elements into a single entity and when it is linking two distinct entities (as in *how* *many adults and how many children*) or processes (as in *admitted . . . and collected . . .*).

Another challenge in this text is the noun group *the price of admission*, an abstraction of the more everyday expression *It costs $?? to get into the museum*. *The price of admission* is also a **nominalization** of the process *admitted* in the first clause (see Chapters 2 and 3 for more on nominalization). Nominalization occurs often in mathematics word problems, and students can learn to link these abstract noun groups with the processes that they repackage (e.g., the verb *admit* → the noun *admission*).

A further linguistic feature of this problem is the **being** process (*is*) in the third clause. A **being** process can describe *attributes* of a participant, as in *The admission price is high*, or define a participant, as in *The admission price is $4*. In this case, the process defines the price of admission, providing the information about how much it costs for adults and children to be admitted to the museum. Again, an ellipsis occurs here; the word *is* is not repeated (e.g., *The price of admission* **is** *$6 for an adult and* **is** *$4 for a child*). Students need to recognize that there are two different grammatical participants involving quantity in this clause and that there are two different mathematical entities to be worked with.

Finally, the information in the circumstances needs to be understood as referring to the same event. In this case, students need to recognize that *on that day* in the final clause refers to the same circumstance as *in one day* in the first clause. **References** such as demonstratives (e.g., *that, this*) and pronouns (e.g., *she, they*) allow the writer to establish cohesive links to prior information (and sometimes to upcoming information). Recognizing the links these references establish helps students keep track of the grammatical participants in the text.

QUESTION 3: WHICH MATHEMATICAL CONCEPTS ARE INDICATED OR SIGNALED IN THE INFORMATION?

Once students have identified the key information given in the text, the next step is to relate that information to the mathematical concepts they have learned. The text information identified in answering Question 2 can be linked with the mathematical concepts needed to solve the problem, as shown in the chart.

INFORMATION PROVIDED IN THE TEXT	MATHEMATICAL CONCEPTS INVOLVED
Clause 4 **Participant:** unknown number of adults; unknown number of children **Process:** were admitted **Circumstance:** into the museum on that day	**Clause 4** **Variable 1** (number of adults) **Variable 2** (number of children)
Clause 1 **Participant:** the National Civil Rights Museum **Process:** admitted (**doing** process) **Participant:** 321 adults and children **Circumstance:** in one day	**Clause 1** **Total number of people admitted** (321 adults and children together)
Clause 2 **Participant:** the National Civil Rights Museum **Process:** collected (**doing** process) **Participant:** $1,590	**Clause 2** **Total amount of money collected** ($1,590)
Clause 3 **Participant:** the price of admission **Process:** is (**being** process) **Participant:** $6 for adult and $4 for child	**Clause 3** **Single ticket price for adult** ($6) **Single ticket price for child** ($4)

The task that has been identified in analyzing Clause 4, finding *how many adults and how many children were admitted on one day,* points to the mathematical concept **unknown variables.** Because the unknown variables concern quantities, we look at the information provided in the text for concepts that involve numbers.

The wording may need to be "translated" from the text information to mathematical concepts. When a mathematical concept is presented as a noun or noun group, the translation is straightforward, as these examples show:

TEXT	→	CONCEPT
$6 for an adult		Single ticket price for adult
$4 for a child		Single ticket price for a child

In other instances, the translation may require transformation of processes into noun groups:

TEXT	→	CONCEPT
admitted 321 adults and children		Total number of people admitted
collected $1,590		Total amount of money collected

The most challenging translation involves turning linguistic cues such as *how many* into the mathematical concept unknown variable:

TEXT	→	CONCEPT
how many adults		Variable 1
how many children		Variable 2

QUESTION 4: WHAT ARE THE MATHEMATICAL PRINCIPLES NEEDED TO USE THE CONCEPTS TO ANSWER THE QUESTION?

In this step, students represent the mathematical concepts identified in Question 3 with appropriate mathematical symbols and/or visual displays and link them with relevant mathematical operations (e.g., theorems, formulas, or equations), as shown.

MATHEMATICAL CONCEPTS IDENTIFIED	MATHEMATICAL PRINCIPLES TO FOLLOW
	Principle 1: The mathematical concepts need to be translated into mathematical symbols and equations.
Variable 1 **Variable 2**	Unknown variables are represented by letters or other symbols: variable 1 = x; variable 2 = y Let x = number of adults admitted Let y = number of children admitted
Total number of attendees	Total number of attendees = $x + y = 321$
Single ticket price for adult	$6 thus, total amount of money collected from adults = $ per adult x number of adults = $6x$
Single ticket price for child	$4 thus, total amount of money collected from children = $ per child x number of children = $4y$
Total amount of money collected	Total amount of money collected = $ from adults + $ from children = $6x + 4y = 1{,}590$
	Principle 2: To obtain values for x and y, two equations need to be solved simultaneously. $x + y = 321$ $6x + 4y = 1{,}590$

QUESTION 5: WHAT PROCEDURES DO I FOLLOW TO USE THOSE
PRINCIPLES IN SOLVING THE PROBLEM?

To answer Question 5, students need to draw on their knowledge about mathematical operations (see the chart on p. 74). Note that there are different ways to solve the problem; one of several possible methods is presented here.

EQUATIONS	PROCEDURES FOR SOLVING THE EQUATIONS
Equation 1: $x + y = 321$ Equation 2: $6x + 4y = 1{,}590$	Step 1: Find the value of x in terms of y from Equation 1. $\quad x = 321 - y$ Step 2: Replace x in Equation 2 with $321 - y$. $\quad 6(321 - y) + 4y = 1{,}590$ Step 3: Find the numerical value of y by solving the above equation. $\quad 1{,}926 - 6y + 4y = 1{,}590$ $\quad y = 168$ Step 4: Find the numerical value of x by substituting 168 for y in Equation 1. $\quad x + 168 = 321$ $\quad x = 321 - 168 = 153$

QUESTION 6: AS A RESULT OF THESE PROCEDURES, WHAT IS THE SOLUTION?

The answer to Question 6 is the end product of the mathematical operations performed in answering Question 5. The solution needs to be aligned with the task, finding _How many adults_ and _how many children were admitted to the museum on that day?_ When addressing Question 4, we have decided to:

> Let x = number of adults admitted
> Let y = number of children admitted

Thus, the numerical value of x and y as the end product of Question 5 is the solution:

> <u>153 adults</u> and <u>168 children</u> were admitted to the museum on that day.

QUESTION 7: HOW CAN I JUSTIFY THE SOLUTION? (DOES THE SOLUTION MAKE SENSE?)

To evaluate and verify the solution, students need to rely on both the information explicitly provided in the text and the mathematical schema

SOLUTION/CHOICE	JUSTIFICATION

$x = 153$
 $y = 168$
	Information from the text:
	     Total number of attendees: 321
	     Total amount of money collected: $1,590
	
	 Information from the mathematical equations:
	     $x + y = 321$
	     $6x + 4y = 1,590$
	
	 Plugging the solutions into the equations:
	 For total number of people admitted: $\underline{153} + \underline{168} = 321$
	 For total amount of money collected: $6 \times \underline{153} + 4 \times \underline{168} = 1,590$
	 Thus, the solutions are correct.

they have retrieved and applied, going back to the word problem as well as using mathematical equations. This is shown here.

Solving a word problem in algebra requires that students first comprehend the language of the problem and then mobilize the relevant mathematics. It is understanding the language of the problem that enables students to make decisions about what mathematical schema to call up and what mathematical knowledge to apply.

Solving a Word Problem in Geometry

Prove: A mid-segment of a triangle (on a co-ordinatized plane) is parallel to the third side and one-half the length of the third side. (From *Discovering Geometry*, p. 683)

QUESTION 1: WHAT IS THE PROBLEM TO BE SOLVED?

Unlike the algebra example, the task to be performed in this problem is presented as a command, not a question. The process **prove** is typical of geometry and requires students to justify the validity of a claim, using argument or evidence. In order to "prove," students need to identify the information that is given (Question 2) and then translate that information into relevant mathematical concepts (Question 3) before evoking relevant principles and procedures to follow (Questions 4 and 5) in finding the answer (Question 6) and justifying it (Question 7).

QUESTION 2: WHAT RELEVANT INFORMATION IS PROVIDED IN THE TEXT?

Students need to reformulate this problem into a multisemiotic configuration involving not only language but also mathematics symbolism and visual display, the three meaning-making resources needed to find and present solutions in geometry (O'Halloran, 2003). Analyzing the participants and attributes, processes, and circumstances identifies the relevant information provided in the text, as shown.

CLAUSES	INFORMATION PROVIDED
1. *A mid-segment of a triangle on a co-ordinatized plane is parallel to the third side (of the triangle).*	**Participant:** *a mid-segment of a triangle on a co-ordinatized plane* **Process:** *is* **Attribute:** *parallel to the third side (of the triangle).*
2. *and (a mid-segment of a triangle on a co-ordinatized plane) (is) one-half the length of the third side (of the triangle).*	**Participant:** *(a mid-segment of a triangle on a co-ordinatized plane)* **Process:** *(is)* **Attribute:** *one-half the length of the third side (of the triangle).*

There are two clauses here, each presenting a mathematical claim (or proposition) to be proved. The ellipsis in both clauses makes the problem concise, but the ellipsed noun group (*a mid-segment of a triangle on a co-ordinatized plane*), verb (*is*), and prepositional phrase (*of the triangle*) in Clause 2 need to be recovered. In addition, the meanings in the complex noun group *a mid-segment of a triangle on a co-ordinatized plane* need to be unpacked and understood. Using the strategy presented in Chapter 2, this long noun group can be deconstructed as follows:

PRE-MODIFIER	*a* (how many)	
HEAD	*mid-segment* (thing)	
POST-MODIFIERS	*of a triangle* (whose)	*on a co-ordinatized plane* (where)

The words *mid-segment, triangle, co-ordinatized,* and *plane* are technical terms, part of the mathematics that students need to know. Unlike in the algebra problem, the **being** processes here construct attributes, describing the *mid-segment* in terms of its position *(parallel to the third side)* and length *(one-half the length of the third side)*, rather than constructing a definition of it. Understanding these attributes is important to constructing an accurate visual representation of the problem.

QUESTION 3: WHICH MATHEMATICAL CONCEPTS ARE INDICATED OR SIGNALED IN THE INFORMATION?

Students next need to translate the key information into mathematical concepts. This requires that they know the definitions of the key technical terms *mid-segment, mid-point, triangle, coordinate,* and *length,* as well as that the attribute *parallel to* signals the concept *two lines with equal slopes,* as shown.

INFORMATION PROVIDED IN THE TEXT	MATHEMATICAL CONCEPTS INVOLVED
Clause 1 **Participant:** a mid-segment of a triangle on a co-ordinatized plane	**Mid-segment:** a line segment that joins the midpoints of two sides of a triangle **Mid-point:** the point halfway between two end points in a line segment **Triangle:** a polygon with three sides and three angles that may be represented as XYZ with each letter representing an angle (vertex of the triangle) **Coordinate:** location of a point on a plane expressed as Q (a, b) where a and b are integers (signed numbers)
Process: is **Attribute:** parallel to	**Parallel lines:** lines that are co-planar and have the same slope **Slope:** inclination of the line
Participant: the third side (of the triangle).	
Clause 2 **Participant:** (a mid-segment of a triangle on a co-ordinatized plane) **Process:** is **Attribute:** one-half the length of the third side (of the triangle).	**Length:** the amount of space between two points

QUESTION 4: WHAT MATHEMATICAL PRINCIPLES ARE NEEDED FOR SOLVING THE TYPE OF GIVEN PROBLEM?

Students need to use the mathematical concepts identified in answering Question 3 to construct a visual display, organizing the information in a tangible way to help solve the problem (see the chart on p. 79). For convenience related to the fact that N is mid-point, K is labeled 2b, 2c instead of b, c, and A is labeled 2a, 0 instead of a, 0.

QUESTION 5: WHAT PROCEDURES DO I FOLLOW TO USE THOSE PRINCIPLES IN SOLVING THE PROBLEM?

To answer Question 5, students need to use the visual display and mathematical formulas and draw on additional mathematical knowledge (see the chart on p. 80). The language of the word problem does not suggest the steps to be taken to solve it, so students have to decide what to do based on the mathematics they have learned.

QUESTION 6: AS A RESULT OF THESE PROCEDURES, WHAT IS THE SOLUTION?

Usually, the answer to Question 6 is the end product of the mathematical operations performed in the previous step (Question 5). However, when it comes to doing a proof, the solution is already stated in the problem, so students' justification is the logical proof. This means that students can move directly to Question 7.

QUESTION 7: HOW CAN I JUSTIFY THE SOLUTION? (DOES THE SOLUTION MAKE SENSE?)

To justify the solution, students need to rely on both the information provided in the text and their mathematical knowledge. However, as opposed to the algebra problem, where the information used to address Questions 6 and 7 comes directly from the text and the solutions, the justification process in this geometry example draws on the mathematical concept (i.e., *slope*) that is signaled in the phrase *parallel to* and on the mathematical symbols provided by the visualization of the word problem (e.g., AK, MN, a, b, c). The identification of relevant concepts and the construction of a visual display, both dependent on understanding the language of the word problem, are crucial for justifying the solution. The chart on page 81 illustrates this justification process.

MATHEMATICAL CONCEPTS IDENTIFIED	MATHEMATICAL PRINCIPLES TO FOLLOW
Mid-segment Mid-point Triangle Coordinate Parallel line Slope Length	**Principle 1: The mathematical concepts need to be translated into visual display with mathematical symbols that provides information in a mathematically tangible way.**

Visualization of the problem provides the information in a tangible manner:

y-axis

K(2b, 2c)

N

O(0, 0)   M   A(2a,0)   x-axis

Triangle AOK with M and N as the mid-points of segment AO and segment KO, respectively.

Vertex O is located at the origin of a co-ordinatized plane.

Choose vertex A (2a, 0) so that one side is on the x-axis, and point K (2b, 2c), a, b, c are real values that will allow any rational-valued coordinates to be expressed this way.

Principle 2: To prove line MN is parallel to line AK, the mid-point formula and the formula for slope are to be used.

- In general, the mid-point formula for any segment EF, where E (a, b) and F (c, d):

  $(\frac{1}{2}[c - a], \frac{1}{2}[d - b])$;

- In general, the formula for slope of any line EF, where E (a, b) and F (c, d):

Slope of any line EF = $(d - b) / (c - a)$

Principle 3: To prove MN = ½AK, the distance formula is to be used.

- In general, the distance formula for any segment PQ, where P = (x_1, y_1) and Q = (x_2, y_2):

$$\sqrt{(x_1 - x_2)^2 + (y_1 - y_2)^2}$$

VISUAL DISPLAY	PROCEDURES FOR WORKING THROUGH THE VISUALIZED PROBLEM
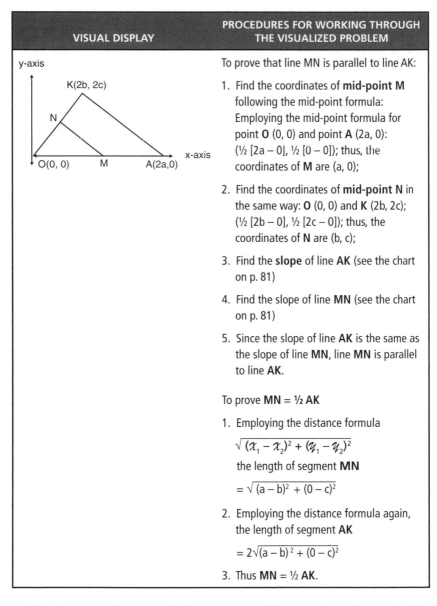	To prove that line MN is parallel to line AK: 1. Find the coordinates of **mid-point M** following the mid-point formula: Employing the mid-point formula for point **O** (0, 0) and point **A** (2a, 0): (½ [2a − 0], ½ [0 − 0]); thus, the coordinates of **M** are (a, 0); 2. Find the coordinates of **mid-point N** in the same way: **O** (0, 0) and **K** (2b, 2c); (½ [2b − 0], ½ [2c − 0]); thus, the coordinates of **N** are (b, c); 3. Find the **slope** of line **AK** (see the chart on p. 81) 4. Find the slope of line **MN** (see the chart on p. 81) 5. Since the slope of line **AK** is the same as the slope of line **MN**, line **MN** is parallel to line **AK**. To prove **MN = ½ AK** 1. Employing the distance formula $$\sqrt{(x_1 - x_2)^2 + (y_1 - y_2)^2}$$ the length of segment **MN** $$= \sqrt{(a-b)^2 + (0-c)^2}$$ 2. Employing the distance formula again, the length of segment **AK** $$= 2\sqrt{(a-b)^2 + (0-c)^2}$$ 3. Thus **MN = ½ AK**.

Proving a mathematical claim or proposition requires clear articulation of the logical connection between the proving process and the resulting solution. Students may need assistance in developing the language needed to present their justifications. In this case, conjunctions are an important language resource for presenting logical reasoning, as the conjunctions *since* and *thus* are used in this justification process.

SOLUTION/CHOICE	JUSTIFICATION
Proposition 1 (slope): **The slope of line AK** = $(2c - 0) / (2b - 2a) =$ $2c / 2(b - a) = $**c / (b - a)**; **The slope of line MN** = $(c - 0) / (b - a) =$ **c / (b - a)**. Proposition 2 (length): **The length of segment MN =** $\sqrt{(a - b)^2 + (0 - c)^2} = \sqrt{(a - b)^2 + c^2}$; **The length of segment AK =** $\sqrt{(2a - 2b)^2 + (0 - 2c)^2} = \sqrt{2^2[(a - b)^2 + c^2]} =$ $2\sqrt{(a - b)^2 + c^2}$	Since **the slope of line AK is the same as the slope of line MN**, thus line **MN** is parallel to line **AK**. Since the length of segment **AK** is twice the length of segment **MN**, thus **MN** = ½ **AK**.

WORKING WITH STUDENTS

The preceding set of seven questions can guide students through the process of solving word problems. These questions are not always followed linearly, as students may go back to previous questions at any stage. For instance, at Question 5, while trying to use the information provided in the text to solve the problem, students may realize that some pieces of information are missing, in which case they may need to go back to Questions 3 and 4. Questions 6 and 7 can also be reversed, depending on whether students are evaluating the options of procedures before reaching a solution (i.e., $7 \rightarrow 6$) or verifying a solution after the solution is reached (i.e., $6 \rightarrow 7$). The flow chart presented in Figure 4.1 captures the recursive nature of this problem-solving process.

It is in addressing the first two questions that the functional language analysis is most helpful. Specifically, analysis of mood (whether the problem asks questions or makes commands) allows students to identify the task they are being asked to do. The analysis of the clause into participants, attributes, processes, and circumstances enables them to identify key information (and the problem situation) in the text and relate it to mathematical concepts. Analysis of **being** processes helps them recognize what is defined or described. Information that has been left out through ellipsis can be recovered as the clauses are analyzed, and attention to conjunctions can help students both understand the

FIGURE 4.1
Sequential but Recursive Process for Using the Seven Guiding Questions
to Solve Word Problems in Mathematics

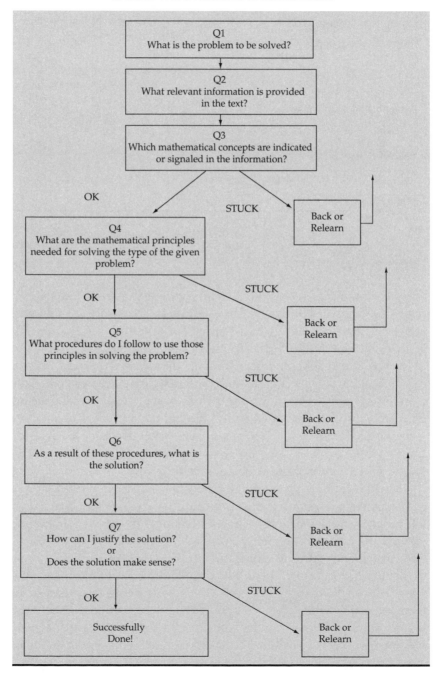

TABLE 4.1

Summary of Key Linguistic Features in Selected Algebra and Geometry
Word Problems

Questions	Linguistic Features
1. What is the problem to be solved?	• questions • commands • conjunctions
2. What relevant information is provided in the text?	• technical vocabulary • complex noun groups • nominalizations • ellipsis • references (demonstratives, pronouns) • **being** processes • conjunctions

problem and present its solution. Tracking the references helps students see where information is related to prior text. Table 4.1 summarizes the language features that can be the focus of attention during the first two stages of the problem-solving process.

Solving a word problem involves both linguistic knowledge and mathematical knowledge, and the seven questions offer a useful heuristic for helping students focus both on language and mathematics. This begins with deconstructing the language to identify the problem to be solved and the information provided so that the relevant mathematical concepts, principles, and procedures can be brought to bear. Mathematics texts are often challenging to read, and functional language analysis goes beyond key words to help students recognize how language works together with mathematical symbols, equations, and graphics to construct mathematical meanings. In today's high-stakes testing environment, many students who know the mathematics principles and constructs are blocked from demonstrating that knowledge because of the language. Functional language analysis enables students to gain access to the ways mathematics word problems are constructed, helping those challenged by the language to find ways to truly demonstrate their knowledge of mathematics.

chapter 5

Reading Literary Texts: Beyond Personal Responses

ANNABELLE LUKIN

> Our way into most of the meanings of most texts is obviously
> through their language: texts after all are linguistic objects, and
> a literature text is no exception to this rule. But in the study of
> verbal art the need to pay attention to language goes beyond
> this. It is not that there is art, and the job of language is simply
> to express it; rather it is that if there is art, it is because of how
> language functions in the text. In everyday life, we all know
> people who can tell a story well and others who just 'kill it'. What
> causes the difference? It is the way the story is 'discoursed', the
> manner in which the patterns of language function to create
> the fable. This analogy is simple, and verbal art is a complex
> phenomenon; none the less, it does point to an important fact
> that in verbal art the role of language is central. Here language
> is not as clothing is to the body; it **is** the body.
> —Hasan, 1985, p. 91, emphasis in original

The language arts teacher has many responsibilities, but a central one
is to engage students in the study of a variety of literary texts. A literary text can be studied in different ways, but no matter how teachers
approach it, at some point they will be involved in helping students
connect the language of the text to an interpretation of the work. In the
study of poetry, for instance, it would be typical to approach a poem

through a search for poetic devices or figurative language, inviting students to look for features such as metaphors, similes, assonance, or alliteration. As significant as these forms can be, they are not enough. For one thing, these devices are not particular to literary texts. Pick up any newspaper and you will find examples of metaphors, similes, or alliteration. Although we refer to these as poetic devices, they in no way define the language of literature. In addition, many writers and poets do not use these devices. One high school teacher made the following comment during an interview:

> I find it a bit unfortunate that . . . we teach them simile and metaphor and everything and they get used to sort of identifying them and discussing what the poet is comparing things to and whether it's effective or not. And they get used to using language that describes vividness or whatever and then we study a poet who doesn't use any of those things, and then they say, "I can't find any of those things; it's not poetry, there are no similes here."

Such an approach encourages students to see literary criticism as a search for particular poetic moments in a text, as if these devices are responsible for its literary quality. Not only is this problematic when such forms are not used by a writer, but it raises questions about how one builds an interpretation of a literary text based on evidence of only selected words, phrases, or sentences. If only particular points in a text are considered worthy of comment, then what of the rest of the text?

Functional language analysis offers an alternative approach to the study of literature in which the literary text is treated as a linguistic object like any other text. Developing earlier work in the structuralist and stylistic traditions (e.g., Jakobson, 1987; Mukarovsky, 1964, 1997; Tynanov, 1978) and drawing on systemic functional linguistics (e.g., Butt, 1996; Halliday, 1971; Hasan, 1985, 1996; Lukin, 2003a; O'Toole, 1982), the approach recognizes that the language of literature is the same language we use to do our shopping, catch up with friends, and write scientific papers. It engages with the special character of literature by seeing that it is not the use of poetic language, but the way writers turn the stuff of ordinary language to aesthetic ends, that gives literature its particular character. As Hasan has argued, "the search for the language **of** literature is misguided; we should look instead at language **in** literature" (1985, p. 94, emphasis in original).

Functional language analysis of literature is explored here in an untitled sonnet by the great American poet Edna St. Vincent Millay (see p. 88). Analyzing various linguistic patterns as a means of arriving at a commentary on the poem can give students who might find literature, and poetry in particular, a little daunting a practical way to get started, without feeling that they need some special intuition to analyze literature. Functional language analysis develops students' sense of the language system in general and asks them to apply that knowledge to a particular literary text. What distinguishes this approach from others is that it stays close to the language of the text and assumes that the form of the language is part of the meaning of the poem.

As a contrast to this approach, consider this excerpt from an essay on Millay's poetry offered to students by an English professor at the University of New Mexico:

> The double standard that restricts women while compelling men to be overtly sexual is ridiculed in Millay's [I, being born a woman and distressed]. The tone of the poem is detached and unemotional, stereotypically masculine. In contrast, the choice of diction keeps the sexual expressions subtle and indirect; the word choice in lines three through five, "Am urged by your propinquity to find / Your person fair, and feel a certain zest / To bear your body's weight upon my breast," is purposely and stereotypically feminine. Concluding physical attractiveness and the convenience of nearness to be practical catalysts for sexual liaisons is part of a logic that has long been associated with males exclusively. The speaker exercises her femininity in a tongue-in-cheek fashion to undo her opponent with the etiquette based on this masculine logic. Using direct dialogue, albeit one-way, the speaker makes it clear to a past conquest that she is not only uninterested in resuscitating their former affair, but coldly adds that she would like this conversation to be their last. (Source: Retrieved January 9, 2008, from www.unm.edu/~aobermei/Eng200/samplepapers/assignment4montg/index.html)

This essay relies on reference to general notions of tone and diction, which are then classified as masculine and feminine, respectively—although the basis for the claims remains opaque, with a direct quote from the poem supposedly the only evidence necessary. The last two sentences of the excerpt are no more than a paraphrase, again supported only by a direct quote from the poem (not included in this excerpt). This is of course just one essay—although its features are found in a range of literary criticism, including Leavis and Bloom (Lukin, 2003b). It is a kind of critique that makes judgments and puts forth interpretations without providing a way for students to see how the interpretation was made. The excerpt quotes the poem but says nothing about the linguistic choices through which Millay created this particular poem. And yet, as Hasan (1985) has suggested, it is the language choices that give the poem its meaning and its force. Helping students recognize these choices and how they work enables them to construct interpretations that are grounded in the language of the text and that do not rely on intuitions that their experiences with literature may not have provided them.

There are many kinds of language patterns in any text that contribute to the meaning: patterns in the **graphology** (layout) and **sound** systems, in the **choice of words**, and in the **grammar**. Patterns of all of these kinds can be investigated, starting with the most obvious—the patterns in the graphological and sound systems. Word choices can then be considered through a **cohesion** analysis to reveal patterns of meaning, followed by analysis at the **clause** level that further delves into the grammar. Patterns in the grammar are the hardest to bring out because they operate beneath our conscious radar and require some special attention. The grammatical patterns are relevant to the study of literary texts because they are resources for simultaneously creating meaning about experience **(experiential meaning)**, meaning about social relationships **(interpersonal meaning)**, and meaning that creates textual coherence **(textual meaning)**. As these language patterns are analyzed, an interpretation of the findings is suggested, which enables the reader to accumulate evidence toward the theme of a literary text.

ANALYZING A POEM

The selected Millay poem was written in 1923 and is one of her many sonnets. First, let's consider the kind of context this poem creates. This is an important starting point because it provides a frame within which to conduct the more detailed analysis of the language features. The poem involves an address to a lover about the nature of their relationship. Clearly, gender is significant: The speaker is female, and we can assume the addressee is male—otherwise the femaleness of the speaker would not be relevant. From this brief summary these questions arise: *What is the speaker saying to her lover? How is their relationship depicted? What sense does the poem communicate about the two lovers?*

I, being born a woman and distressed

By all the needs and notions of my kind,

Am urged by your propinquity to find

Your person fair, and feel a certain zest

To bear your body's weight upon my breast:

So subtly is the fume of life designed,

To clarify the pulse and cloud the mind,

And leave me once again undone, possessed.

Think not for this, however, the poor treason

Of my stout blood against my staggering brain,

I shall remember you with love, or season

My scorn with pity,—let me make it plain:

I find this frenzy insufficient reason

For conversation when we meet again.

Source: *Collected Sonnets* by Edna St. Vincent Millay. New York: Harper and Row, 1988, p. 41, Sonnet VIII. Reprinted with permission.

PATTERNS IN GRAPHOLOGICAL AND SOUND SYSTEMS

To begin the linguistic investigation of the poem, let's work from some obvious features, such as how the poem looks on the page. This is important because the relationship of the text to the page is one of the defining features of poetry. Together with patterns in rhyme and rhythm, the organization of a poem into lines and stanzas is a deep part of the artistry in a poem, perhaps particularly in the case of concrete or visual poetry, where typographic resources and layout are self-consciously taken up by poets as modes of meaning.

From the perspective of the graphological system, then, students note first the pattern of lines and stanzas, as well as what the use of punctuation might indicate. The poem has 14 lines in a single stanza. The number of lines is indicative of its status as a sonnet, although the number of lines alone does not define a sonnet. Indeed, the function of a sonnet is to present an "observation and conclusion, or statement and counter-statement" (Fuller, 1972, p. 2), which suggests we should find evidence of two parts to the poem. Sometimes, this is signalled through a stanza break, but not in this case. If we consider the punctuation, we see that the poem consists of two sentences, the first taking up the initial eight lines, and the second running over the final six lines. These sentence boundaries thus reinforce the idea of the poem coming to us in two moves. These two moves are further indicated by the rhyme scheme, which is *abba cddc* for the first eight lines, and then *efefef* for the final six lines. About halfway through each sentence, we find a colon, a punctuation mark indicating a relationship of equivalence. What comes after the colon is considered a restatement of what has come before.

Thus, from observing fairly simple patterns, students can see something of the rhetorical organization of the poem: it has two global moves—representing the observation and conclusion, or statement and counter-statement function of the sonnet—each of which is organized around an apposition, an "i.e." structure (see Figure 5.1). How these two

FIGURE 5.1
Graphological and Sound Patterns of the Sonnet

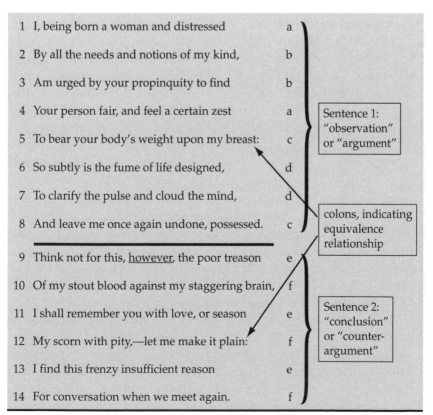

moves are related to each other is indicated in the conjunction *however* in Line 9, which suggests an adversative relationship between the two moves in the poem.

From the perspective of sound patterning, the rhyme scheme and its contribution to the construction of the two moves in the poem has already been recognized. Note also that, as is traditional in the sonnet form, the poem has five beats per line, and is therefore a pentameter. If we were able to hear the poem read aloud, we would also be able to consider the role of intonation in the performance of the poem.

Analyzing the choices of punctuation, line and stanza, and rhyme and rhythm is a concrete way into the textual organization. It allows students to see easily observable, but quite significant, patterns, including the form and rhetorical organization of the poem into its two-part structure of observation and conclusion, as well as the internal organization of each of these moves.

PATTERNS IN WORD CHOICE: A COHESION ANALYSIS

Moving from graphology and sound patterns, let's consider the effect of patterns of wording through a cohesion analysis that tracks the word choices line by line in the poem. **Cohesion** is created mainly through references such as pronouns and demonstratives, lexical items (content words) that are semantically related in some way, and conjunctions (Halliday & Hasan, 1976). The cohesion analysis in Table 5.1 focuses on references and lexical items, taking the content words and pronouns and tracking chains of words that have a semantic affinity through the poem. Content words related as synonyms or antonyms, or through other relationships such as part-whole relations, appear in each column. Only the more extended chains of related words are shown because they help reveal the dominant semantic fields or motifs of the poem. The items that appear in parentheses are ellipsed in the original text, but need to be retrieved by the reader. For instance, in *Let me make it plain*, the reader understands the one who is to let her make it plain is *you*. For the purposes of tracking these participants, the ellipsed forms are brought back into the analysis and indicated by parentheses.

The cohesion analysis shows the poem is organized around two central characters, the speaker and the addressee. The speaker has a higher profile in the poem relative to the addressee, since there are 11 references to her (excluding *we*) and only six to her lover. The poem is therefore much more concerned with the *I* than the *you*. And there is only one point at which the two become *we*, at the end of the poem. The effect of

TABLE 5.1
Cohesion Analysis of Millay Poem

Line No.	Speaker	Emotion	Body	Intellect	Addressee
1	I	distressed			
2	my		needs	notions	
3				find	your
4		feel, zest			your
5	my		body, breast		your
6				designed	
7			pulse	mind	
8	me	undone, possessed			
9				think	(you)
10	my, my		blood	brain	
11	I (I)	love		remember	you
12	my, me	scorn, pity			(you)
13	I	frenzy		find, reason	
14	we				we

this is that despite their sexual relationship, the speaker constructs the two as individuals and not as a couple.

Table 5.1 also shows three other consistent semantic chains in the text, titled emotion, body, and intellect. These chains indicate that one of the preoccupations in the poem is the battle between the emotions/body and the intellect: for instance, *to clarify the pulse and cloud the mind* and *my stout blood against my staggering brain*. For the speaker, there is a conflict between her emotional and physical feelings—which she suggests are a function of her gender—and her intellectual reasoning, a conflict that is resolved in the second move of the poem.

THE POEM IN CLAUSES

Further grammatical analysis involves looking at the poem in terms of clauses. Traditional grammar contains main clauses and dependent clauses. The main clause can stand alone, while the dependent clauses depend on the main clause and cannot stand alone. For instance, *being born a woman* or *to find your person fair* do not have sufficient grounding to stand on their own. They have little interactional power; their function is to expand on the main clause. The main clauses in the poem are indicated in bold type in Table 5.2. A clause can also interrupt another, and the clause beginning the poem is interrupted by the second and third clauses, indicated by the chevron brackets (<< >>). Finally, a clause can be embedded inside another clause—that is, it can be part of another constituent in a clause. Clause 5 *and feel a certain zest [[To bear your body's weight upon my breast:]]* involves an **embedded clause**, which is indicated by the double square brackets ([[ ]]). The embedded clause forms part of the noun group *a certain zest . . .* , with the embedded information functioning to define which *zest* the speaker is talking about (see Chapter 2 for more on embedded clauses).

TABLE 5.2
The Sonnet in Clauses

Clause No.	Clause
1	**I, << >>, Am urged by your propinquity**
2	<<being born a woman
3	and distressed By all the needs and notions of my kind>>
4	to find Your person fair,
5	and feel a certain zest [[To bear your body's weight upon my breast:]]
6	**So subtly is the fume of life designed,**
7	To clarify the pulse
8	and cloud the mind,
9	And leave me once again undone, possessed.
10	**Think not for this, however, the poor treason Of my stout blood against my staggering brain,**
11	I shall remember you with love,
12	or season My scorn with pity,
13	**—let me make it plain:**
14	**I find this frenzy insufficient reason For conversation**
15	when we meet again.

Seeing the poem in clauses allows us to consider the grammatical choices in the poem with respect to a number of points of view. First, we can ask what the grammar reveals about the kind of social interaction taking place, looking at the clause from the perspective of **interpersonal meanings.** Second, we can look at the **experiential meanings,** the kind of experience being constructed. Finally, we can examine choices about the organization of each clause, considering which elements come first and the effect of this on the overall information delivery, the **textual** meanings of the clause.

EXPLORING INTERPERSONAL MEANINGS

Exploring the grammar of interaction—the grammar for taking up speech roles in an exchange—reinforces the first observations about the poem: it is an address by a woman to her lover. There are two characters, but only one speaks. In general terms, when we are engaged in interaction, we take up a speech role and are involved in an exchange. What we exchange is either information as we question (demand) or state something (give), or goods and services as we offer (give) or command (demand). Each interactive unit, then, is one of four basic speech function types: **giving information (statement), demanding information (question), giving goods and services (offer),** or **demanding goods and services (command),** as illustrated in Table 5.3.

Speech function is a characteristic of main clauses, in combination with any dependent clauses elaborating or enhancing the main clause. This role is marked in every main clause, so in Millay's poem, Clauses 1, 6, 10, 13, and 14 can be analyzed for their speech function value. Of these, Clauses 6 and 14 are giving information, while Clauses 1, 10, and 13 are commands. The commands of Clauses 10 and 13 are directed to the lover, while Clause 1 is a softened command, in which her lover's propinquity *urges*—rather than commands—the speaker to find him *fair* and *to feel a certain zest to bear your body's weight upon my breast*. The commands in Clauses 10 and 13 come in the second move of the poem—as part of the conclusion or counterstatement—and they have a very direct feel about them; the speaker is not trying to hide her feelings or soften the blow for her lover.

TABLE 5.3
Typical Grammatical Forms of the Speech Functions

	Information	Goods and Services
Give	Give + information = statement	Give + goods & services = offer
	Typical grammatical form is the declarative mood: *I'm having a drink.*	No typical grammatical form associated with offer. It is expressed by a range of forms: imperative (*Have a drink!*), interrogative (*Would you like a drink?*), declarative (*I'll get you a drink.*)
Demand	Demand + information = question	Demand + goods & services = command
	Typical grammatical form is the interrogative mood: *When are we having a drink?*	Typical grammatical form is the imperative mood: *Bring me a drink!*

To explore this further from the perspective of **mood**, a main clause is one of a small number of types: declarative, interrogative, or imperative. The names of these mood types echo speech functions. Thus, **declarative** is the form associated with statements, the **interrogative** with questions, and the **imperative** with commands (see Table 5.3). Part of the directness of the commands by the speaker to her lover comes from the use of the imperative form. This is important to note because a command does not have to come in the imperative form. We often command others in much less direct ways through declaratives (e.g., *I'd like you to close the door*) or interrogatives (e.g., *Would you mind closing the door?*). At the same time, the imperative form does not equal a command since the imperative can express speech functions other than command (e.g., *Let me get you a drink!*). Therefore, these two instances of the speaker commanding her lover through the imperative indicate something about the nature of this relationship. Given the content of these commands, these grammatical forms suggest that the speaker is taking up a position of power relative to the addressee. One further point about these commands: the use of the more archaic *think not* rather than the modern usage *Don't think that . . .* gives the poem the feel of an Elizabethan sonnet. The formality of this more archaic usage contrasts strongly with the directness of the second of these commands, *let me make it plain*. The contrast gives a particular force to the second command, suggesting that whatever indecision there might have been earlier in the poem has been unambiguously resolved for the speaker.

A further feature of the directness of this address is the absence of modality. **Modality** is a general term that includes **modal verbs** like *may*, *might*, or *would,* as well as related words like *maybe, probably,* or *possibly.* These words are used when there is some uncertainty, such as when a situation is not black and white. The speaker in this poem uses no modality whatsoever, indicating that her views are categorical.

EXPLORING EXPERIENTIAL MEANINGS

To explore the experiential meanings of the poem, we can look at the clauses from the point of view of the processes and participants, or who does what to whom, how, when, where, and why. Processes can be classified as types of **doing, being, sensing,** or **saying.** By looking at the process types in a text, we can ask: *Is the text about acting, sensing, saying, or states of being?* And given that we have identified two central figures in the poem, the speaker and the addressee, an exploration of process type can help students determine how these characters are configured—do they both act, think, say, and exist (be)? Table 5.4 presents a process type analysis for Millay's poem, with the processes (verbs) indicated in bold.

Table 5.5 includes all the clauses labelled as **doing** processes, and the final column lists the grammatical **Actor**—the entity with responsibility for the action. From this list, we can see first of all that the lover is only an Actor as part of the *we* in Clause 15 in an action that is not yet actualized. Apart from her role as part of the *we* in Clause 15, the speaker is Actor twice. In Clause 5.1, she is the Actor in the only action that directly refers to the sexual act. This is a significant selection, as it makes her—the female—the one doing the doing in the description of sex. She is also the Actor in Clause 12, in which she is commanding her lover not to think that she will *season her scorn with pity*. This leaves Clauses 6 through 8. In Clause 6, the Actor—the entity responsible for designing *the fume of life*—is left unspecified. In Clauses 7 and 8, we find *the fume of life* as the entity that *clarif[ies] the pulse and cloud[s] the mind*. In these three clauses, the poet effectively makes a metaphysical statement about how life and love come to be the way they are and, in so doing, takes away human

---

TABLE 5.4
Process Type Analysis for Millay's Poem

Clause No.	Clause	Process Type
1	I, << >>, **Am urged** by your propinquity	saying
2	<<**being born** a woman	being
3	and **distressed** By all the needs and notions of my kind>>	sensing
4	**to find** Your person fair,	being
5	and **feel** a certain zest [[5.1 **To bear** your body's weight upon my breast:]]	sensing [[5.1 doing]]
6	So subtly **is** the fume of life **designed**,	doing
7	**To clarify** the pulse	doing
8	and **cloud** the mind,	doing
9	And **leave** me once again undone, possessed.	being
10	**Think** not for this, however, the poor treason Of my stout blood against my staggering brain,	sensing
11	I shall **remember** you with love,	sensing
12	or **season** My scorn with pity,	doing
13	—let me **make** it plain:	being
14	I **find** this frenzy insufficient reason For conversation	being
15	when we **meet** again.	doing

TABLE 5.5
Doing Process Clauses in Millay's Poem

Clause No.	Clauses with Doing Processes	Process	Actor
5.1	[[to bear your body's weight upon my breast]]	bear	(I)
6	So subtly is the fume of life designed,	design	unspecified
7	To clarify the pulse	clarify	(the fume of life)
8	and cloud the mind,	cloud	(the fume of life)
12	or season My scorn with pity,	season	(I)
15	when we meet again.	meet	we

responsibility for the state of the relationship. In other words, it is not her lover who clouds her mind and causes her pulse to race, but rather some general state of affairs that is part of being human.

The next table (5.6) presents the poem's four clauses that construe mental experience, showing the **Senser** for each clause—that is, the entity that undergoes the mental experience—and the **Phenomenon**—that which is felt/thought by the Senser or causes the mental experience. Again, the speaker is a much more dominant character than the addressee, who turns up in Clause 10 as a Senser in a negated process. As previously noted, this clause also is a command—thus the speaker asserts for herself the right to tell her lover what (not) to think. Two of the **sensing** process clauses are about feelings—the processes *distress* and *feel*—and concern the feelings of the speaker. Of the lover's feelings we know nothing. The cause of the speaker's distress is *the needs and notions of my kind*, and the source of her feeling *a certain zest* is *your propinquity*, which turns up in the only **saying** process clause in the poem: *I <<. . .>> am urged by your propinquity. . .*(Clause 1). The lover is absent as a **Sayer** in the poem. Only his *propinquity*—his nearness—urges her to find him fair. In what is a further insult, his *propinquity* is a characteristic that is temporary and shared by others. In other words, it is not some feature unique to her lover that brings on her feeling *a certain zest*.

Finally, the poem involves processes of **being.** As the term suggests, these processes describe states of being. In this poem, they involve some entity—called the **Carrier**—who is ascribed a characteristic of some kind—called the **Attribute**. For example, in the clause *She is happy*, *She* is the Carrier and *happy* is the Attribute. The typical verb in the **being** processes is *to be*. But it is not always this verb, and in some cases, the verb *be* is left out, as in *She made me happy*. The relationship between *me* and *happy* is a relational one—that is, *I was happy*—but in this formu-

TABLE 5.6
Sensing Process Clauses in Millay's Poem

Clause No.	Clauses with Sensing Processes	Process	Senser	Phenomenon
3	and (I) (being) distressed by all the needs and notions of my kind	distress	(I)	all the needs and notions of my kind
5	and feel a certain zest [[…]]	feel	(I)	a certain zest [[…]]
10	Think not for this, however, the poor treason Of my stout blood against my staggering brain,	think	(you)	-
11	I shall remember you with love,	remember	I	you

lation, the **being** process is left out. The role of *She* in this example is **Attributor**—the entity that makes *me* be *happy*. Clauses 9, 13, and 14 are clauses of this kind.

Table 5.7 sets out the five **being** process clauses in the poem. The first, from the opening lines, gives the characteristic of *woman* to the speaker, signalling the importance of gender in this poem. She later (in Clause 9) describes herself as *undone, possessed*—a state of being brought on by *the fume of life*. In this clause, *me* is the Carrier, while *the fume of life* is the Attributor—the entity ascribing the Attribute to the Carrier. The lover is also the Carrier of an Attribute—he is described as *fair*, in the clause *to find your person fair* (Clause 4). In this case, the speaker is the source, or Attributor, of this characteristic, although at the urging of his *propinquity*. In Clause 14, we have the description of *this frenzy* as *insufficient reason for conversation*. In this clause we again have the role Attributor, taken up by the speaker. As we have found in the other grammatical selections, the speaker has prominence in this grammatical function, giving her a more dynamic role in the relationship, relative to the addressee, since he is overlooked for this grammatical role. Thus, he never makes her "be" anything. In Clause 9, where she is *undone, possessed*—a deeply emotional state—the Attributor is not her lover, but *the fume of life*.

EXPLORING TEXTUAL MEANINGS

One final grammatical analysis is looking at the clauses from the point of view of the choices involved in the ordering of elements in a clause. Take for instance the first clause of the poem, *I . . . am urged by your propinquity*. In this example, the writer has elected to begin the clause with *I*. In doing so, she makes *I* the point of departure for the clause, or the

TABLE 5.7
Being Process Clauses in Millay's Poem

Clause No.	Clause	Process	Carrier	Attribute	Attributor
2	being born a woman	be born	I	a woman	-
4	to find your person fair	find	your person	fair	(I)
9	and leave me once again undone possessed	leave (be)	me	undone, possessed	(the fume of life)
13	let me make it plain	make (be)	it	plain	me
14	I find this frenzy insufficient reason For conversation	find (be)	this frenzy	insufficient reason For conversation	I

Theme. As with Chapters 2 and 3, the term *Theme* (with a capital *T*) is treated here as a grammatical category signalling the choice the writer makes about what comes first in a clause. We need to keep this use of Theme distinct from the widely used sense of the "theme" (with a lower case *t*)—or deep meaning—of a literary work. The significance of a writer's choice of Theme lies in the fact that alternatives are available. For instance, Millay could have written *Your propinquity urges me . . . .* In this alternative, *Your propinquity* is the Theme of the clause.

Some kinds of dependent clauses do not allow for alternative choices in the ordering of elements, so these clauses cannot be analyzed for Theme. A clause such as *to find Your person fair*, for instance, has no Theme because there is no other element that could come first in the clause. Thus, no choice has been exercised over the ordering of elements; the ordering is determined by the status of the clause. Table 5.8 presents a Theme analysis for the Millay poem, the dash indicating clauses with no Theme. The Theme analysis reinforces what we have seen already in this poem: the dominance of the speaker. What the Theme analysis adds is that the typical orientation to clauses in this poem is the speaker.

REVIEWING THE FINDINGS OF THE ANALYSIS

From this analysis, there is no doubt that the female speaker in this poem is asserting herself in a most direct fashion. From an interpersonal point of view, she is the only speaker: she both declares and commands through the most direct of grammatical forms, the imperative, and she uses no

TABLE 5.8
Theme Analysis of Millay Poem

Clause No.	Theme	Clause No.	Theme
1	I,	9	-
2	-	10	Think
3	-	11	I
4	-	12	(I)
5	-	13	- let me
6	So subtly	14	I
7	-	15	when we
8	-		

modality, which signals she has no uncertainty about her message. From the experiential analysis, the speaker is also the dominant character: she acts, she thinks and feels, and she attributes. Her lover, meanwhile, is grammatically marginalized. His only power comes from his *propinquity*, and not through any special characteristic of him as an individual. He does not take action—even in the sexual act—and we are given no sense of his thoughts or feelings. And he says nothing, except what is communicated by his *propinquity*. Whatever she feels is the consequence of *the fume of life*, rather than any action or characteristic of her lover. The battle between her emotions/physical feelings and her intellect is thus entirely internal—it is a battle she has with herself and her nature, one in which he has very little part to play. From a textual point of view, the poem is organized largely around the speaker, since *I* or *me* is typically the point of departure.

Let's now return to the two-part structure of the poem and consider it in relation to the findings from the grammatical analyses. The first part establishes the grounds of the argument: the state of play of the relationship from the speaker's perspective in the context of her nature as a woman, subject to the *needs and notions of my kind*—which is all part of *the fume of life*. The second move in the poem rejects the relationship and divests the addressee of any romantic fancy he may harbor. The final couplet clinches this rejection, a powerful culmination of the accumulating marginalization of her lover as a person of any significance in her life.

WORKING WITH STUDENTS

To analyze a poem, students can move through different orders of language organization. They can begin with patterns in the graphological and sound systems—the expression levels of language—since it is through these means that language is processed as writing or speech. They can then look at patterns in the words and grammar, examining the language from the interpersonal, experiential, and textual angles. In all these analyses, they can draw on evidence from the language to make observations about the meaning of the text as well as its rhetorical organization.

EXPLORING PATTERNS IN GRAPHOLOGY AND SOUND

Graphological patterns are an obvious place to start in poetry, given the importance of line as a poetic resource. Students can begin by checking the basic distribution of line and stanza in relation to sentence boundaries and, if relevant, consider these patterns in relation to the poetic form. This can be represented diagrammatically. A diagram of these relationships also allows students to see whether sentences are short or long and to consider the effect of sentence length on the pacing and complexity of the poem. Poets often play with a range of graphological features—line and stanza relations or font—for an added visual effect, and this kind of poetry can be used to instruct students in the use of graphological features for poetic ends. Turning to sound patterns, students can consider the role of rhyme and meter, and, where there is interest in the spoken performance of a poem, the role of intonation in creating an additional kind of meaning.

EXPLORING PATTERNS IN WORDS AND GRAMMAR

A cohesion analysis can illuminate some crucial semantic veins in a poem, and given that it involves simply tracking related words and expressions, it is a reasonably straightforward mode of analysis. Working with the unit of clause makes it possible to explore some of the deeper grammatical features of a text. From an interpersonal point of view, students can look at a text in relation to the grammar of mood: Is the poem monologic or dialogic? Does it involve declaratives, interrogatives, or imperatives? Are there different characters in the poem? What kinds of speech roles are they given? In addition, is there modality? If so, what is the effect? From an experiential point of view, the poem can be analyzed, clause by clause, for its process types. This will show whether the poem is about **doing, thinking, saying,** or states of **being.** Each clause can then be analyzed in terms of the kinds of participants: Are they human or non-human, and what range of grammatical roles do they take up? From a textual point of view, who or what is typically Theme in the poem, and what does this reveal about the poem's preoccupations?

EXPLORING PATTERNS OF MEANING

Getting at the meaning of a poem is what motivates any literary study. Functional language analysis is especially useful for students because it uses linguistic evidence as a basis for exploring a poem. The approach enables students to build up a case about the meaning from the exploration of various kinds of language patterns that all make meaning. In this case, the examination of line, punctuation, and rhyme scheme revealed the two global moves of the poem and their relationship, as well as the internal structure of each of these moves. The cohesion analysis revealed dominant motifs in the poem. The study of speech function, mood, and modality showed the nature of the interaction and the way the speaker constructed the relationship. The experiential patterns—patterns of process types and participants—showed why the speaker is so dominant in the poem, and the Theme analysis showed the centrality of the speaker as the point of departure.

Functional language analysis is also relevant to other literary genres (see Hasan, 1985, on point of view in prose). Table 5.9 presents the kinds of analysis, language resources, and questions that students can ask in doing functional language analysis of poems. Using this table as a guide, students can find a way to make claims about meaning grounded in detailed textual evidence. This approach contrasts with the earlier example of an essay on Millay's poetry that offered interpretations either without evidence or using only paraphrase or direct quotes as evidence.

In reading this poem, most teachers would naturally explore its form as a sonnet, including its rhyme scheme and division into two moves. What is new about functional language analysis is that it focuses on the actual language of the text by promoting systematic explorations of language patterns, where grammar is interpreted as a meaning-making resource. The analysis of grammar requires special effort because it is complex. But learning to see grammatical organization in language, particularly by being able to identify clauses and to see various kinds of meaning in them, enables students to develop a significantly new capacity for analyzing literary and other texts.

Functional language analysis also removes the pressure on students to be intuitive about the theme of a poem. While students are often

TABLE 5.9

A Guide to Functional Language Analysis of Poems

Kinds of Analysis	Language Resources	Questions
Graphology and Sound Systems	page layout, line, stanza, sentence boundaries, punctuation, rhyme, rhythm	• How many lines and stanzas? • What is the relationship of sentence boundaries to line/stanza? • Is there a rhyme scheme? • Is the poem metrical? • Are sentences long or short?
Words	cohesion patterns (lexical and referential chains)	• Are there developed lexical fields in the poem? • What do these patterns suggest about the motifs in the poem?
Grammar: Interpersonal	speech function, mood, modality	• Is the poem monologic or dialogic? • What speech functions do you find in the poem? • How are they expressed? • Is there modality?
Grammar: Experiential	process patterns, participant patterns	• What kinds of processes are there? (doing, sensing, saying, or being?) • What kinds of participants are there? • Are they human or non-human?
Grammar: Textual	Theme	• Who or what has prominence by coming first in the clause?
Rhetorical Organization	poetic form, rhetorical structure	• Is the poem written in a particular poetic form? • Is there some kind of rhetorical structure through which the poem unfolds? • How does the overall organization of the poem relate to the other kinds of patterning in the poem?

urged to produce a personal response to a literary work, the reality of assessment means that only particular kinds of responses are valued in school. It is not the case that any personal response will do. Functional language analysis enables students to go beyond personal response and engage with the poem as a linguistic artifact. Using this explicit approach to the study of a literary text does not mean all students will arrive at the same conclusions; for instance, the way individual students will evaluate the stance taken by the speaker in Millay's poem will vary. But by working with the actual language of a text, students learn about the way language works and can also come to see what it means to use the forms and structures of language for aesthetic ends.

chapter 6

Functional Language Analysis in the Classroom

> The exploration of language can be the most exciting pursuit in the whole curriculum.
>
> —Halliday, 2007b, p. 57

The functional language analysis approach presented in this book can help teachers more effectively address the reading demands of the secondary school curriculum and enable students to participate more fully in the literacy practices that characterize each academic subject. Each chapter has highlighted key issues in the ways language works, offering concrete strategies for approaching the texts in a particular subject. At the same time, the chapters as a whole have illustrated a way of talking about language that can work across subjects as students reflect on the language choices an author has made in constructing a text. Functional language analysis provides teachers with a language for talking about language that is accessible even to those without a background in language analysis. It is a linguistically responsive approach that can help teachers work more effectively in today's secondary school classrooms, where multilingual and multicultural students bring varied backgrounds, experiences, and language proficiencies. But this approach is not just for the struggling reader. Even the best of our students gain new insights when they have tools for engaging with text and talking about the ways language organizes knowledge and embeds particular perspectives.

It was suggested in Chapter 1 that all teachers, regardless of their subject area, read all of the chapters in this book because each chapter can illustrate only a limited picture of the way texts work in each discipline. Reading about other subjects can fill out the picture and help teachers engage with a wider range of texts, as teachers of each subject use texts of greater variety than we have been able to demonstrate in a single chapter. Science classes, for example, may use texts that describe historical accomplishments in science or chronicle the life of a scientist in ways similar to the way history is written. Sometimes mathematics may require that students read explanations similar to those used in science. In history, students work with a wide range of text types, so reading about texts in other subjects can help history teachers engage with language different from the textbook passage and primary source text in Chapter 3. Likewise, language arts teachers work with a variety of text types and may find that texts presenting literary analyses draw on the kind of explanation structure discussed in the science and history chapters, where Thematic progression builds an interpretation, aided by nominalization, abstraction, and complex noun groups.

Each text example also connects in some way with the texts students read in other disciplines, so the analyses in each chapter offer insights to guide functional language analysis across school subjects. The science explanation, for example, has features of expository text more generally, with its tightly knit structure that builds a theory through a flow of information from Rheme to Theme. The three patterns of history text, presenting a sequence of events, juxtaposing points of view, and arguing for a particular perspective, can also be found in other subjects. The framework for analyzing mathematics word problems can be applied to short exam-type questions outside of mathematics, and other texts that have not been constructed primarily for pedagogical purposes can be approached through the comprehensive analysis illustrated in the language arts chapter. For all teachers, understanding the language analysis strategies presented throughout this book can provide useful insights for engaging students with a range of texts.

SEEING MEANING IN GRAMMAR

Functional language analysis strategies offer students ways to engage with the language of advanced literacy, enabling them to recognize how meaning is presented in complex patterns of grammar so that they can read and write like scientists, historians, mathematicians, novelists, and other content specialists. The language of secondary school disciplines has developed over time to meet new needs and purposes, and the everyday language that serves adolescents well in their daily lives does not suffice for understanding and constructing the kinds of texts that present the specialized knowledge of secondary school mathematics, science, social studies, and language arts.

To talk about language and how it works to construct meaning, a functional metalanguage has been developed throughout this book. This "language for talking about language" enables students and teachers to focus on the meaning in the language patterns commonly used in secondary school texts. Drawing on this metalanguage, teachers can be explicit about how language constructs knowledge and value in their subject and raise students' awareness about the experiential, interpersonal, and textual meanings in language. As students focus on the language that constructs the text they are reading and discussing, they learn to see the patterns of language that also appear in other texts in the subject area, giving them tools and strategies for better independent reading and writing. The language analysis strategies that have been presented across the chapters are:

- Explore the **experiential meaning** by analyzing **processes, participants**, and **circumstances** in a clause (Chapters 2, 3, 4, and 5) and by analyzing **conjunctions** (Chapters 3 and 4) and **lexical and referential chains** (Chapter 5).

- Explore the **interpersonal meaning** by analyzing **mood** and **modality** (Chapters 4 and 5) and by recognizing how an author construes value and interpretation in **process types** and in the meanings presented in particular **participants** and **circumstances** (Chapters 2, 3, and 5).

- Explore the **textual meaning** by tracing the development of information in **Theme/Rheme** structuring (Chapters 2, 3, and 5), by identifying where **cohesive devices** are used (Chapters 2, 3, 4, and 5), and by recognizing the condensation of information in **nominalizations** and **noun groups of varying complexities** (Chapters 2, 3, and 4).

Since every clause presents experiential, interpersonal, and textual meanings that contribute to the overall purpose of a text, we need functional interpretations of language. The power of the functional grammar is in linking structure with meaning. Functional language analysis is not just mechanical labeling of language structures. While language is, of course, made up of nouns, verbs, prepositions, adjectives, adverbs, and conjunctions, these are not meaning-based categories. Labeling with these grammatical word class names does not offer students any insights into the relationship between the grammar and the meaning of a text. The functional terminology, on the other hand, puts the focus directly on meaning. But the traditional word class terms are not unrelated to the functional terms, and for teachers already comfortable using the traditional categories, seeing this relationship can be useful. Table 6.1 shows how the functional grammar terms relate to the traditional grammatical word class categories, and how they relate to the three kinds of meaning explored in this book.

As Table 6.1 shows, every language constituent is involved in construing experiential, interpersonal, and textual meanings. The language of functional grammar puts the focus on meaning and shows how the meanings typically associated with the word class terms can also be constructed in alternative ways. These alternative ways of expression are common in secondary school texts. For example, although processes are typically expressed in verbs, a process can also be expressed in a noun through nominalization. Logical connections, while typically expressed in conjunctions, can also be expressed in verbs and nouns. The functional language analysis focuses attention on the grammatical meaning rather than the grammatical word class. Experiential meaning can be explored when the focus of the discussion is on the main idea, and this can be done principally through the different process types and their associated processes, participants, attributes, and circumstances. An exploration of interpersonal meaning can be emphasized when it is important to establish the power positioning of characters in a text, the social relationship between author and reader, or the interpretive perspective being presented in a text, focusing on the various ways different grammatical word class elements function to construe these role relationships and attitudes. Exploration of textual meaning, where all of the traditional word classes are involved, helps readers recognize text structure and the evolution of ideas.

Showing how the functional labels relate to the traditional word classes, as Table 6.1 does, only illuminates part of the power of the functional language analysis approach, however. The real power comes from the broader focus the approach allows by enabling students to recognize how meaning evolves from clause to clause in a text. Going beyond the clause-level metalanguage of participants, processes, and circumstances, students can look at experiential, interpersonal, and textual meanings in the context of a text as a whole, using functional linguistics constructs

TABLE 6.1
Relating Functional Grammar to Traditional Grammar

Functional Categories	Grammatical Word Class Terms	Role in Meaning-Making
Processes	Typically realized in verbs and verb groups but sometimes in nouns and noun groups (i.e., nominalizations)	• Experiential meaning: construing doing, sensing, saying, being • Interpersonal meaning: construing mood (declarative, interrogative, imperative) and modality (obligation, possibility, usuality, etc.) • Textual meaning: nominalization of processes helps construct information flow and develop argument in a text
Participants	Typically realized in nouns and noun groups	• Experiential meaning: construing semantic roles (e.g., Actor, Senser) • Interpersonal meaning: construing interactional roles (e.g., giving, demanding) • Textual meaning: often presenting Themes that show the method of development in a text; creating cohesive links and chains of meaning through references (pronouns, demonstratives), synonyms, antonyms, and other semantic relationships
Circumstances	Typically realized in prepositional phrases and adverbs	• Experiential meaning: construing time, place, manner, etc. • Interpersonal meaning: construing affect, attitudes, judgments, etc. • Textual meaning: functioning as Themes that indicate the method of development in a text
Qualities	Typically realized in adjectives	• Experiential meaning: construing attributes • Interpersonal meaning: construing judgment and attitude • Textual meaning: adding information to complex noun groups
Logical Connections	Typically realized in conjunctions	• Experiential meaning: construing logical reasoning • Interpersonal meaning: signaling judgments • Textual meaning: constructing cohesive links within the text

such as process types, Thematic progression, cohesion, logical connection, and speech function to explore content, interpretation, evaluation or relationship, and text organization.

FUNCTIONAL LANGUAGE ANALYSIS IN CLASSROOM INSTRUCTION

Good teaching incorporates a variety of classroom activities. Functional language analysis is only one of many pedagogical practices that make content accessible to students, and it should be embedded in a sequence of activities in which students listen, speak, interact, and do project work in a coherent unit of instruction. It adds depth to students' understanding of the disciplinary content and values presented in texts of different types and provides incentives for students to read for meaning and to articulate their insights and critiques about the texts they read. The approach offers a contemporary, linguistically informed way of tackling academic texts, enabling teachers to engage students in productive discussion about meanings in text that complements other instructional activities to support content learning.

Not all meaning in a text can be determined through analysis of the language choices. The multisemiotic resources (language, symbols, visual representation) highlighted in the mathematics chapter are found to varying degrees in many of the texts students read. Orthographic (titles, headings, bold print, italics) and non-language (photos, charts, and other visuals) elements contribute to meaning in the texts students read in all subjects. Moreover, understanding the meaning of a text requires being able to relate it to other texts or experiences that students have engaged with. But each unit of instruction inevitably involves interaction with texts of some kind. As students read content area texts, engaging in functional language analysis helps them recognize how the particular language choices give the text its meaning potential. By deconstructing and talking about challenging texts, teachers and students see how authors use language to present meaning in discipline-specific ways. Table 6.2 offers a set of questions that can be asked in analyzing a text, along with some analysis strategies that help answer them.

The functional language analysis approach can be implemented with different texts throughout the school year. It can be used in reading textbooks, trade books, primary source documents, test items, and other texts where language analysis can help students construct meaning from difficult language. Its focus is not on analysis for its own sake, but analysis to get at the meanings that enable students to learn content and

TABLE 6.2
Text Questions and Corresponding Analysis Strategies

Questions about Text	Functional Language Analysis Strategies
How is this text organized?	• Analyze patterns of Thematic progression • Analyze process types • Analyze cohesive devices
What is this text about? Who does what to whom, how, when, and where?	• Analyze clause participants and attributes, processes, and circumstances
What is the author's perspective, and how is that perspective infused into the text?	• Analyze process types and participant roles • Analyze word choice
What information is implicit or missing from this text?	• Analyze ellipsis • Analyze conjunction • Analyze nominalization
What are the key concepts or characters developed in this text?	• Analyze lexical and referential chains
How does the author of this text interact with the reader? How do the characters in this text interact with each other?	• Analyze speech functions and mood • Analyze modality

at the same time develop critical-thinking skills. Therefore, when doing functional language analysis, it is less important to get the analysis right than to have a conversation about the analysis with students. Whether, for example, a process is **doing** or **being** is less important than a conversation about how it may be on the borderline between these two meanings and providing an opportunity for students in the classroom to express their views about the meaning they see in the language.

While every teacher can use functional language analysis to explore a text, it is the content area teacher who is uniquely positioned to help students interpret the meanings that are revealed through the analysis and relate them to the larger goals and conceptual frameworks of the discipline. Teachers can use functional language analysis on the spot to help students deconstruct complex or challenging sentences as they read, but a more powerful approach is to incorporate analysis and talk about text into every unit of instruction. Each chapter in this book has suggested many classroom-based activities that enable teachers to apply functional language analysis in a particular content area. A process for infusing text analysis and discussion into content area instruction is described in the following steps:

1. **Select a text.** Functional language analysis calls for close reading and discussion of text, focusing in detail on its structure and meanings. Texts that are worth the time and effort spent on the analysis need to be important and challenging. Usually, it is best to choose a short passage, one that is complete in itself in terms of the ideas it presents. Choose a text that has information that is important but difficult to understand.

2. **Identify goals.** Specify the disciplinary knowledge and concepts that students are expected to develop through analysis of the text. Then, use Table 6.2 to identify questions that correspond to the content objective and select the functional language analysis strategy (or strategies) that can provide answers to these questions.

3. **Analyze the text.** Practice analyzing the text using the functional language analysis strategies. During the analysis, take note of how particular decisions were made in cases where more than one possible answer exists so that you are prepared to answer questions students may have as they engage in the analysis. Think about what the analysis reveals about the text. At times, it may be necessary to try a different analysis strategy to see if it provides additional insights into the meanings in the text.

4. **Introduce the metalanguage.** Introduce students to the particular functional metalanguage they will need to do the text analysis and discussion. Each chapter in this book has introduced a number of metalanguage terms and provided examples where analyses using these terms are applied. Although unfamiliar to students, these metalanguage terms are no more complex or technical than the specialist terminology (e.g., *vowel*, *simile*, *polyhedron*, *chlorophyll*, *constitution*) that populates content area texts. Students will develop both understanding and confidence in using this functional metalanguage if they are provided with explanation, demonstration, and guided practice. Table 6.1 can be used as a reference to help students see how the functional metalanguage terms relate to the traditional grammar terms, as most students are already familiar with the traditional grammar.

5. **Engage students in the analysis.** Many activities that illustrate functional language analysis can be found in this book. These activities can be done individually, in pairs or groups, or as a whole class. They

can occur during reading aloud, guided reading, reading workshop, or reading conference. As students become more comfortable with functional language analysis, they can be asked to apply it on their own during independent reading in school and at home, analyzing texts and reporting on the meanings they see through the analysis.

Using this process, teachers can more effectively engage students in careful deconstruction of text, helping them unpack meaning through conversation about what is included and what is left out of a text, about who is represented and who is not, about who is commanding whom to do what, about what has been compacted and what has been expanded, about whose agency is highlighted and whose is hidden, about how an argument is being developed and what is not developed in the argument, and about the points of view that are constructed as well as the kind of interpretation and explanation an author is presenting. In such discussion, it may become clear that key information for understanding a text is missing or that concepts are not well developed in the text. This provides teachers with important information that can help them enhance the text through additional texts or other activities.

Functional language analysis, then, gives teachers a powerful vehicle for engaging students in thoughtful reading, providing a way of bringing out and critically appraising the information and knowledge students are expected to learn. But the value of the approach goes beyond comprehension instruction. It can be used for other **curricular and assessment purposes** as well, including evaluating and developing curriculum materials, informing writing instruction and assessment, and offering consistent language development across subjects and grade levels. For example, functional language analysis can help teachers **evaluate the difficulty level of students' reading materials.** Traditional readability formulas can be misleading in their assessment of text difficulty because of their limited focus on number of words or syllables and sentence length. Teachers can use functional language analysis strategies to assess the complexity of noun groups and density of information, to look at the way information is structured in a text, and to evaluate how implicit the reasoning or agency is. These are sources of reading difficulty that go beyond the number of words and sentence length. Using functional language analysis, teachers can also better **match texts to students' reading abilities** and prepare reading materials and design assignments that meet the needs of particular groups of students.

Functional language analysis can also **inform writing instruction** by helping teachers be proactive in focusing on language structures that students may not already be using in their writing. The meaning of conjunctions and various options for structuring text, for example, can become a focus of instruction when assigning writing tasks, rather than waiting to respond to what students have already written. Many adolescent learners face challenges in learning to write for academic purposes, and functional language analysis enables teachers to focus their students' attention on features of the texts they read as models of how to present information in more academic and discipline-specific ways. Teachers can show students how to pack more information into noun groups, use nominalization to develop cohesive texts that flow, deploy abstractions to articulate their points of view and make arguments, and include **being** processes to construct technical taxonomies and attribute qualities. Showing students how these grammatical resources construct meanings not only extends students' awareness of language but assists them in developing proficiency in using academic language to read and write like scientists, historians, mathematicians, novelists, and others who engage with contexts of advanced literacy.

Teachers can also use the constructs of functional grammar, rather than intuitions or vague rubrics, to **establish concrete criteria for evaluating students' academic writing.** For example, when evaluating students' science reports or explanations, teachers can look for evidence of students' ability to use noun groups of varying complexities to effectively pack information into a clause, or use nominalization to condense meanings and develop a chain of reasoning. Analysis of students' choice of Themes can help teachers evaluate how effectively the text organization serves its purpose (e.g., to chronicle events over time or to construct an explanation). Ultimately, understanding how language is used and varies across text types and disciplines can help teachers make their expectations related to school-based tasks transparent for students, offering principled and systematic ways of tracking students' writing development. Because much of adolescent students' school learning is evaluated through written language, explicitness about what is expected of language use is important. With functional language analysis, teachers can more clearly articulate their expectations for course assignments and help students see how their language choices construct valued or less valued responses.

Schools and programs can likewise **gain greater consistency in presenting expectations and responding to students** by adopting the functional metalanguage and analysis strategies across subjects and grade levels. The shared terminology can provide a common language for students as they move from one subject area to another and from one grade level to the next, allowing for more effective use of instructional time and promoting more productive discussion about texts. This enhances student learning of subject content while also promoting collaboration and inquiry among teachers.

All school subjects are dependent on language for learning and understanding. Secondary school students have to be able to read difficult texts in order to engage in the activities that enable them to develop new understanding of complex and technical materials. This is a difficult challenge, particularly for struggling readers and students learning English as a second language. While teachers can provide students with classroom experiences that help make some of these challenging materials come alive, ultimately, to deal with the abstract concepts and interpretations that are needed to learn academic subjects, students need language resources. They need to learn to recognize the patterns of language that construct knowledge and values in different ways in different subjects so that they can more effectively engage in the advanced literacy tasks of generalization, computation, theorization, abstraction, explanation, exposition, and reflection. The challenge for teachers of adolescents is to know how to work with texts in ways that help students recognize these language patterns and develop discipline-specific literacies. This is not just a question of having good intentions. Teachers also need knowledge about and skills in teaching discourses to which students have not yet gained access or in which they are not yet proficient. The functional language analysis approach we have presented in this book helps teachers develop this expertise, offering them a new tool for enabling adolescent learners to participate more effectively in the discourses and contexts of secondary schooling and beyond.

APPENDIX:
STUDY GUIDE FOR THE BOOK

The functional language analysis approach presented in this book involves many linguistic constructs and analytical strategies. These constructs and strategies are introduced gradually as they become relevant to the analysis of texts in particular content areas. Table A presents an overview of functional language analysis. It suggests questions that can be asked and answered through functional language analysis, indicating the relevant language patterns that can be analyzed and where the

TABLE A:
A GUIDE TO FUNCTIONAL LANGUAGE ANALYSIS

Questions Asked by the Reader	Language Patterns to Analyze	Chapters Illustrating the Analysis
How is the text organized?	Theme and Rheme structure, process types, construction of time and cause	Chapters 2, 3, 4, & 5
How can dense and abstract sentences in the text be unpacked?	noun group structure, nominalization	Chapters 2, 3, & 4
What is the text about? Who does what to whom, how, when, and where?	participant, attribute, process, and circumstance	Chapters 2, 3, 4, & 5
What is the author's perspective and how is that perspective infused into the text?	process types, nominalization, word choice	Chapters 2, 3, & 5
What information is implicit or missing from the text and how can it be recovered?	reference, ellipsis, conjunction, nominalization	Chapters 2, 3, 4, & 5
What are the key concepts or characters developed in a text?	lexical and referential chains	Chapter 5
How does the author interact with the reader, or how do characters in the text interact with each other?	speech function, mood, modality	Chapters 4 & 5
How can the vocabulary challenges of a text be identified?	technical vocabulary	Chapters 2 & 4
How can the informational density of different texts be compared?	lexical density	Chapter 2

analyses are introduced and exemplified in the book. This table can be used as a reference when reading the book and applying the functional language analysis approach in teaching and learning.

In addition, the chapter-by-chapter questions can be used to guide discussion about the central thesis in each chapter and application of functional language analysis strategies in the content area and grade level of interest.

GUIDING QUESTIONS

Chapter 1
- What are the challenges facing secondary teachers today?
- Why is the phrase "literacy across the curriculum" problematic? Why is it more appropriate to talk about "content area *literacies*" rather than "content area *literacy*"?
- Why are content area teachers best positioned to foster content area literacies?
- What are the three kinds of meaning that are simultaneously present in any text?
- What are the current approaches to teaching reading in secondary content areas? Why is a functional language analysis approach needed?

Chapter 2
- Identify four key features of science discourse. How are these features constructed linguistically? How does understanding these features contribute to the development of science literacy and scientific habits of mind?
- Chapter 2 describes two kinds of technical vocabulary. Examine a text from your content area. Does it use words that are specifically coined for and unique to your field? Does it use everyday words with specialized meanings? Which of these do you think would be most challenging for students?
- Chapter 2 describes how nominalization and abstraction work in science. Examine a text from another content area or from another science topic. Do you find nominalization and abstraction? Compare your text with the texts that your colleagues or classmates are analyzing. Which kinds of texts seem to have the most nominalization and abstraction? Does the nominalization and abstraction result in suppression of agency, as described in Chapter 2? If so, why might that be functional in the particular text you are analyzing? Why has the author adopted that strategy?
- Calculate the lexical density of your text and compare it with the texts of your classmates or colleagues. Which kinds of texts are most lexically dense? Which linguistic elements contribute most to a text's lexical density?
- Sample a few texts from different grade levels. Calculate their lexical density. Compute the readability scores of these texts using one of the readability formulas that are available on the Internet (e.g., Fry, Raygor, Flesch-Kincaid, Dale-Chall, SMOG). Then compare the lexical density and readability indices of these texts and think about which index seems to provide the most accurate measure of a text's reading difficulty level.

■Compare noun groups in different types of texts across different genres and subject areas. In which kinds of texts are they most complex? What do you think this complexity is achieving?

■Analyze the Theme/Rheme progression in your text. Does it have information that flows from Rheme to Theme? Does it hold the Theme constant? Does it vary in its patterns of information flow? How is this relevant to the overall purpose of the text?

Chapter 3

■How do historians use language as a technology to build in interpretation and facilitate reasoning in the text?

■Choose a textbook from a content area and grade level that you are interested in. Select a chapter and look at the patterns of language across the chapter. Does it vary in the same way as the history text that is analyzed in Chapter 3?

■Use the three questions in Chapter 3 to analyze a section of the chapter you have chosen:

- Analyze the macro-organization and the Themes to think about how the text is organized.
- Analyze the configurations of processes, participants, and circumstances to look at what the text is about.
- Analyze the **doing** and **sensing/saying** processes to identify who the author is presenting as key actors and thinkers/sayers, and analyze the **being** processes to look at what is defined and described and the evaluation the author has built in. Look for causal reasoning in the circumstances, conjunctions, and processes to see how interpretation is infused into the text.

■Is the section you have analyzed similar to the chronicling, point of view, or explanation pattern described in Chapter 3? Does it have a different pattern? If so, how would you characterize the pattern?

Chapter 4

■What is the role of language in comprehending and solving word problems in mathematics?

■Choose some assessment tasks from your content area. These could be short-answer questions, reading comprehension questions, or other short texts. Use the strategies described in Chapter 4 to analyze the assessment tasks and identify the linguistic challenges they present to students.

- Identify the tasks that the students are being asked to do and the specific language that sets those tasks.
- Analyze the information provided in the questions that is relevant for answering them by focusing on the configurations of processes, participants, and circumstances.
- Look at the logic of the texts through analysis of conjunctions. Where is ellipsis used and what information does it require that students recover?

■Identify a high-stakes reading test, and compare the language used in the reading passages and in the comprehension questions. Is there a difference between the way test questions are worded and the way language is used in the reading passages? How might this difference affect students' performance on the test?

Chapter 5
- How is the linguistically oriented approach exemplified in Chapter 5 similar to and different from the reader response approach used in many language arts classrooms?
- Use the approach in Chapter 5 to analyze a short text or section of a text that students typically find challenging. In particular, it is useful to analyze a text that might be open to different interpretations.
- Parse the text into clauses and analyze it from the different perspectives described in Chapter 5. Identify the ways that the particular language choices of the author color the meaning. Think about alternative language choices that might have resulted in a different overall effect.

Chapter 6
- To which areas of curriculum and instruction can functional language analysis be productively applied? Share what you find from these application exercises with colleagues or classmates.
- Use the guidelines in Chapter 6 to engage your colleagues or classmates in close reading of a text through functional language analysis. Have them reflect on what they see in the text before and after the close reading. Consider what you might do differently if you engage students in talk about the text
- Choose a text from your content area and develop a plan to engage students in reading it, following the process described in Chapter 6. If you are teaching, try the lesson with students. Reflect on what they were able to learn about content and language through the functional language analysis activities. In what way does functional language analysis help develop students' critical awareness about text?

General Questions for the Book
- How has functional language analysis helped you understand language and enhance learning in your content area?
- What are some ways that you can go beyond vocabulary instruction in focusing on language in the texts you teach?
- Grammar has traditionally been seen as a set of rules about language use that students are supposed to memorize. In this book, it is described in another way as a resource for making meaning just as a palette of colors is used as a resource for painting by artists. What are the implications that each conception of grammar has for teaching reading and writing?
- What challenges do adolescent readers face that go beyond the challenges of elementary reading? How can functional language analysis help students meet those challenges?
- Recent scholarship on adolescent literacy recognizes that each academic subject has its own ways of using language. This scholarship calls for a focus on discipline-specific reading/writing practices in literacy instruction. How does the functional language analysis approach described in this book enable this focus? In what way does it help promote students' development of multiple literacies across different academic content areas?

REFERENCES

Abedi, J., & Lord, C. (2001). The language factor in mathematics tests. *Applied Measurement in Education, 14*(3), 219–234.

Achugar, M., & Schleppegrell, M. J. (2005). Beyond connectors: The construction of *cause* in history textbooks. *Linguistics and Education, 16*(3), 298–318.

Alvermann, D. (2001). *Effective literacy instruction for adolescents*. Chicago: National Reading Conference.

American Association for the Advancement of Science (AAAS) (1993). *Benchmarks for science literacy*. New York: Oxford University Press.

Anton, H. (1992). *Calculus with analytic geometry* (4th ed.). New York: Wiley.

Austen, J. (1818/1998). *Persuasion*. London: Penguin Books.

Beck, I. L., & McKeown, M. G. (1994). Outcomes of history instruction: Paste-up accounts. In M. Carretero & J. F. Voss (Eds.), *Cognitive and instructional processes in history and the social sciences* (pp. 237–256). Mahwah, NJ: Lawrence Erlbaum.

Beck, R. B., Black, L., Krieger, L. S., Naylor, P. C., & Shabakam, D. I. (2003). *Modern world history: Patterns of interaction*. Evanston, IL: McDougall Littell.

Berman, I., & Biancarosa, G. (2005). *Reading to achieve: A governor's guide to adolescent literacy*. Washington, DC: National Governors Association Center for Best Practices.

Biancarosa, G., & Snow, C. (2004). *Reading Next—A vision for action and research in middle and high school literacy: A report from Carnegie Corporation of New York*. Washington, DC: Alliance for Excellent Education.

Boscardin, K., & Aguirre-Muñoz, Z. (2006). *Consequences and validity of performance assessment for English language learners: Integrating academic language and ELL instructional needs into Opportunity to Learn measures* (No. CSE 678). Los Angeles: National Center for Research on Evaluation, Standards, and Student Testing (CRESST).

Butt, D. (1996). Literature, culture and the classroom: The aesthetic function in our information era. In J. James (Ed.), *The language-culture connection* (pp. 86–106). Singapore: SEAMEO.

Carnine, L., & Carnine, D. (2004). The interaction of reading skills and science content knowledge when teaching struggling secondary students. *Reading & Writing Quarterly, 20,* 203–218.

Cassels, J., & Johnstone, A. (1985). *Words that matter in science*. London: Royal Society of Chemistry.

Chenhansa, S., & Schleppegrell, M. (1998). Linguistic features of middle school environmental education texts. *Environmental Education Research, 4*(1), 53–66.

Christie, F. (1998). Learning the literacies of primary and secondary schooling. In F. Christie & R. Misson (Eds.), *Literacy and schooling* (pp. 47–73). London: Routledge.

Clement, L.A., & Bernhard, J. Z. (2005). A problem-solving alternative to using key words. *Mathematics Teaching in the Middle Grades, 10*(7), 360–365.

Coffin, C. (2004). Learning to write history: The role of causality. *Written Communication, 21*(3), 261–289.

———. (2006a). *Historical discourse: The language of time, cause, and evaluation.* London: Continuum.

———. (2006b). Learning the language of school history: The role of linguistics in mapping the writing demands of the secondary school curriculum. *Journal of Curriculum Studies, 38*(4), 413–429.

Deshler, D., Ellis, E., & Lenz, B. (1996). *Teaching adolescents with learning disabilities: Strategies and methods.* Denver, CO: Love Publishing.

DiGisi, L., & Willett, J. (1995). What high school biology teachers say about their textbook use: A descriptive study. *Journal of Research in Science Teaching, 32*(2), 123–142.

Eggins, S. (2004). *An introduction to systemic functional linguistics* (2nd ed.). London: Pinter.

Fang, Z. (2005a). Thematic analysis as a new tool for genre assessment in early literacy research. *National Reading Conference Yearbook, 54,* 168–181.

———. (2005b). Scientific literacy: A systemic functional linguistics perspective. *Science Education, 89*(2), 335–347.

———. (2006). The language demands of science reading in middle school. *International Journal of Science Education, 28*(5), 491–520.

———. (2008). Going beyond the Fab Five: Helping students cope with the unique linguistic challenges of expository reading in intermediate grades. *Journal of Adolescent and Adult Literacy, 51*(6), 476–487.

Fang, Z., Lamme, L., & Pringle, R. (2009). *Teaching reading, language, and literature in inquiry-based science classrooms, grades 4–8.* Norwood, MA: Christopher-Gordon.

Fang, Z., Schleppegrell, M., & Cox, B. (2006). Understanding the language demands of schooling: Nouns in academic registers. *Journal of Literacy Research, 38*(3), 247–273.

Fisher, D., Brozo, W., Frey, N., & Ivey, G. (2007). *50 content area strategies for adolescent literacy.* Columbus, OH: Merrill.

Fuller, J. (1972). *The sonnet*. London: Methuen.

Guzzetti, B., Hynd, C., Skeels, S., & Williams, W. (1995). Improving physics texts: Students speak out. *Journal of Reading, 38*(8), 656–663.

Halliday, M. A. K. (1971). Linguistic function and literary style: An inquiry into the language of William Golding's *The Inheritors*. In S. Chatman (Ed.), *Literary style: A symposium* (pp. 330–365). New York: Oxford University Press.

———. (1978). *Language as social semiotic*. London: Edward Arnold.

———. (1982). Linguistics in teacher education. In R. Carter (Ed.), *Linguistics and the teacher* (pp. 10–15). London: Routledge.

———. (1993). Towards a language-based theory of learning. *Linguistics and Education, 5*(2), 93–116.

———. (1998). Things and relations: Regrammaticising experience as technical knowledge. In J. R. Martin & R. Veel (Eds.), *Reading science: Critical and functional perspectives on discourses of science* (pp. 185–235). London: Routledge.

———. (2007a). Language across the culture (1986). In J. Webster (Ed.), *Language and education* (Vol. 9, pp. 291–305). London: Continuum.

———. (2007b). Some thoughts on language in the middle school years (1977). In J. Webster (Ed.), *Language and education* (Vol. 9, pp. 49–62). London: Continuum.

Halliday, M. A. K., & Hasan, R. (1976). *Cohesion in English*. London: Longman.

Halliday, M. A. K., & Martin, J. R. (1993). *Writing science: Literacy and discursive power*. Pittsburgh, PA: University of Pittsburgh Press.

Halliday, M.A.K., & Matthiessen, C. (2004). *An introduction to functional grammar* (3rd ed.). London: Arnold.

Hammond, J. (2006). High challenge, high support: Integrating language and content instruction for diverse learners in an English literature classroom. *Journal of English for Academic Purposes, 5*(4), pp. 269–283.

Hand, B., & Prain, V. (2006). Moving from border crossing to convergence of perspectives in language and science literacy research and practice. *International Journal of Science Education, 28*(2/3), 101–107.

Hasan, R. (1985). *Linguistics, language and verbal art*. Geelong, Australia: Deakin University Press.

———. (1996). On teaching literature across cultural differences. In J. James (Ed.), *The language-culture connection* (pp. 34–63). Singapore: SEAMEO.

Heller, R., & Greenleaf, C. L. (2007). *Literacy instruction in the content areas: Getting to the core of middle and high school improvement*. Washington, DC: Alliance for Excellent Education.

Hewitt, P. G. (2002). *Conceptual physics.* Upper Saddle River, NJ: Prentice Hall.

International Reading Association (IRA). (2006). *Standards for middle and high school literacy coaches.* Newark, DE: IRA.

International Reading Association (IRA) and National Middle School Association (NMSA). (2001). *Supporting young adolescents' literacy learning.* Newark, DE: IRA.

Jakobson, R. (1987). *Language in literature.* Cambridge, MA: Harvard University Press.

Jones, L. (2006). *How textbooks influence the formal EE curriculum: A case study.* Paper presented at the annual meeting of North American Association for Environmental Education, Minneapolis, MN.

Kamil, M., & Bernhardt, E. (2004). The science of reading and the reading of science: Successes, failures, and promises in the search for prerequisite reading skills for science. In E. W. Saul (Ed.), *Crossing borders in literacy and science instruction: Perspectives on theory into practice* (pp. 123–139). Newark, DE: International Reading Association.

Kesidou, S., & Roseman, J. (2002). How well do middle school science programs measure up? Findings from Project 2061's curriculum review. *Journal of Research in Science Teaching, 39,* 522–549.

Kintsch, W. (1987). Understanding word problems: Linguistic factors in problem solving. In M. Nagao (Ed.), *Language and artificial intelligence* (pp. 197–208). Amsterdam: Elsevier.

———. (2004). The construction-integration model of text comprehension and its implications for instruction. In R. Ruddell & N. Unrau (Eds.), *Theoretical models and processes of reading* (5th ed., pp. 1270–1328). Newark, DE: International Reading Association.

Lager, C. A. (2006). Types of mathematics-language reading interactions that unnecessarily hinder algebra learning and assessment. *Reading Psychology, 27,* 165–204.

Larson, R., Boswell, L., Kanold, T., & Stiff, L. (2001). *Algebra 1.* Evanston, IL: McDougal Littel.

Leech, G., & Short, M. (1981). *Style in fiction: A linguistic introduction to English fictional prose.* London: Longman.

Leinhardt, G., Stainton, C., Virji, S. M., & Odoroff, E. (1994). Learning to reason in history: Mindlessness to mindfulness. In M. Carretero & J. F. Voss (Eds.), *Cognitive and instructional processes in history and the social sciences* (pp. 131–158). Mahwah, NJ: Lawrence Erlbaum.

Lemke, J. (1990). *Talking science: Language, learning, and values.* Norwood, NJ: Ablex.

References ———————————————————————————123

———. (2003). Mathematics in the middle: Measure, picture, gesture, sign, and word. In M. Anderson, A. Sáenz-Ludlow, S. Zellweger, & V. V. Cifarelli (Eds.), *Educational perspectives on mathematics as semiosis: From thinking to interpreting to knowing* (pp. 215–234). Brooklyn, NY: Legas.

Lock, G. (1996). *Functional English grammar: An introduction for second language teachers*. Cambridge, UK: Cambridge University Press.

Lukin, A. (2003a). Grammar and the study of poetry. In J. James (Ed.), *Grammar and the classroom: RELC anthology* (pp. 228–246). Singapore: SEAMEO.

———. (2003b). *Examining poetry: A corpus-based approach to literary criticism.* Unpublished Ph.D. thesis. Macquarie University, Sydney.

Macken-Horarik, M. (2006). Recognizing and realizing "what counts" in examination English. *Functions of Language, 13*(1), 1–35.

Martin, J. R. (2002). Writing history: Construing time and value in discourses of the past. In M. J. Schleppegrell & M. C. Colombi (Eds.), *Developing advanced literacy in first and second languages: Meaning with power* (pp. 87–118). Mahwah, NJ: Lawrence Erlbaum.

McKenna, B. (1997). How engineers write: An empirical study of engineering report writing. *Applied Linguistics, 18*(2), 189–211.

McKeown, M. G., & Beck, I. L. (1994). Making sense of accounts of history: Why young students don't and how they might. In G. Leinhardt, I. L. Beck, & C. Stainton (Eds.), *Teaching and learning in history* (pp. 1–26). Mahwah, NJ: Lawrence Erlbaum.

Meltzer, J., & Hamann, E. T. (2004). *Meeting the literacy development needs of adolescent English language learners through content area learning. Part one: Focus on motivation and engagement.* Providence, RI: Northeast and Islands Regional Educational Laboratory, Brown University.

———. (2005). *Meeting the literacy development needs of adolescent English language learners through content area learning. Part two: Focus on classroom teaching and learning strategies.* Providence, RI: Northeast and Islands Regional Educational Laboratory, Brown University.

Millay, E. S. V. (1988). *Collected sonnets of Edna St. Vincent Millay.* New York: Harper and Row.

Miller, G. (1967). *The psychology of communication: Seven essays.* Baltimore: Penguin Books.

Modern biology: The dynamics of life. (2006). Columbus, OH: Glencoe/McGraw-Hill.

Mohan, B. (1986). *Language and content.* Reading, MA: Addison-Wesley.

Mohan, B., & Slater, T. (2004). The evaluation of causal discourse and language as a resource for meaning. In J. A. Foley (Ed.), *Language, education and discourse: Functional approaches* (pp. 255–269). London: Continuum.

Moore, D., Bean, T., Birdyshaw, D., & Rycik, A. (1999). Adolescent literacy: A position statement. *Journal of Adolescent & Adult Literacy, 43*, 97–112.

Mukarovsky, J. (1964). Standard language and poetic language. In P. L. Garvin (Ed.), *A Praque School reader on esthetics, literary structure and style* (pp. 17–30). Washington, DC: Georgetown University Press.

————. (1977). *The word and verbal art.* New Haven, CT: Yale University Press.

National Council of Teachers of English (NCTE). (2004). *A call for action: What we know about adolescent literacy and ways to support teachers in meeting students' needs.* Retrieved August 12, 2008, from http://www.ncte.org/about/over/positions/category/read/118622.htm

————. (2006). *NCTE principles of adolescent literacy reform: A policy research brief.* Urbana, IL: NCTE.

National Research Council (1996). *National science education standards.* Washington, DC: National Academy of Science.

Norris, S., & Phillips, L. (2003). How literacy in its fundamental sense is central to scientific literacy. *Science Education, 87*(2), 224–240.

O'Halloran, K. (2003). Educational implications of mathematics as a multisemiotic discourse. In M. Anderson (Ed.), *Educational perspectives on mathematics as semiosis: From thinking to interpreting to knowing* (pp. 185–214). Toronto: Legas.

O'Toole, L. M. (1982). *Structure, style and interpretation in the Russian short story.* New Haven, CT: Yale University Press.

Perie, M., Grigg, W., & Donahue, P. (2005). *The nation's report card: Reading 2005* (NCES 2006–451). Washington, DC: U.S. Department of Education.

Readence, J., Bean, T., & Baldwin, S. (2004). *Content area literacy: An integrated approach* (8th ed.). Dubuque, IA: Kendall/Hunt.

Reif, F., & Larkin, J. (1991). Cognition in scientific and everyday domains: Comparison and learning implications. *Journal of Research in Science Teaching, 28*(9), 733–760.

Rutherford, J., & Ahlgren, A. (1990). *Science for all Americans.* New York: Oxford University Press.

Schleppegrell, M. J. (1998). Grammar as resource: Writing a description. *Research in the Teaching of English, 32*(2), 182–211.

————. (2004). *The language of schooling: A functional linguistics perspective.* Mahwah, NJ: Lawrence Erlbaum.

————. (2005). *Helping content area teachers work with academic language: Promoting English language learners' literacy in history* (Final report: Individual Research Grant Award #03-03CY-061G-D). Santa Barbara: University of California Linguistic Minority Research Institute.

Schleppegrell, M. J., & Achugar, M. (2003). Learning language and learning history: A functional linguistics approach. *TESOL Journal, 12*(2), 21–27.

Schleppegrell, M. J., Achugar, M., & Oteíza, T. (2004). The grammar of history: Enhancing content-based instruction through a functional focus on language. *TESOL Quarterly, 38*(1), 67–93.

Schleppegrell, M. J., & Colombi, M. C. (Eds.). (2002). *Developing advanced literacy in first and second languages: Meaning with power.* Mahwah, NJ: Lawrence Erlbaum.

Schleppegrell, M. J., & de Oliveira, L. C. (2006). An integrated language and content approach for history teachers. *Journal of English for Academic Purposes, 5*(4), 254–268.

Schleppegrell, M. J., Greer, S., & Taylor, S. (2008). Literacy in history: Language and meaning. *Australian Journal of Language and Literacy, 31*(12): 174–187.

Schumm, J. S., Vaughn, S., & Saumell, L. (1992). What teachers do when the textbook is tough: Students speak out. *Journal of Reading Behavior, 24*(4), 481–503.

Science voyages: Exploring the life, earth, and physical sciences (level red). (2000a). Columbus, OH: Glencoe/McGraw-Hill.

Science voyages: Exploring the life, earth, and physical sciences (level green, Florida edition). (2000b). Columbus, OH: Glencoe/McGraw-Hill.

Serra, M. (1993). *Discovering geometry.* Berkeley, CA: Key Curriculum Press.

Short, D., & Fitzsimmons, S. (2007). *Challenges and solutions to acquiring language and academic literacy for English language learners: A report to Carnegie Corporation of New York.* Washington, DC: Alliance for Excellent Education.

Søvik, N., Frostrad, P., & Heggberget, M. (1999). The relation between reading comprehension and task-specific strategies used in arithmetical word problems. *Scandinavian Journal of Educational Research, 43*(4), 371–398.

Thompson, G. (2004). *Introducing functional grammar* (2nd ed.). London: Arnold.

Tynanov, J. (1978). On literacy evolution. In L. Matejka & K. Pomorska (Eds.), *Readings in Russian poetics: Formalist and structuralist views* (pp. 66–78). Cambridge: MIT Press.

Unsworth, L. (2001). *Teaching multiliteracies across the curriculum: Changing contexts of text and image in classroom practice.* Philadelphia: Open University Press.

Vacca, R., & Vacca, J. (2005). *Content area reading: Literacy and learning across the curriculum* (8th ed.). Boston: Allyn & Bacon.

Vande Kopple, W. J. (1994). Some characteristics and functions of grammatical subjects in scientific discourse. *Written Communication, 11*(4), 534–564.

Van de Walle, J. A. (2004). *Elementary and middle school mathematics: Teaching developmentally* (5th ed.). Boston: Allyn & Bacon.

Veel, R. (1997). Learning how to mean—scientifically speaking: Apprenticeship into scientific discourse in the secondary school. In F. Christie & J. R. Martin (Eds.), *Genre and institutions: Social processes in the workplace and school* (pp. 161–195). London: Cassell.

Walker, R. (2003). *Genes & DNA*. Boston: Kingfisher.

Wellington, J., & Osborne, J. (2001). *Language and literacy in science education*. Philadelphia: Open University Press.

Wyndhamn, J., & Säljö, R. (1997). Word problems and mathematical reasoning: A study of children's mastery of reference and meaning in textual realities. *Learning and Instruction, 7*, 361–382.

Yore, L., Hand, B., Goldman, S., Hildebrand, G., Osborne, J., Treagust, D., & Wallace, C. (2004). New directions in language and science education research. *Reading Research Quarterly, 39*(3), 347–352.

Zambo, R. (1994). *Beliefs and practices in mathematical problem solving instruction: K–8*. Paper presented at the Annual Meeting of the School Science and Mathematics Association, Fresno, CA. ERIC ED75006.

ABOUT THE AUTHORS

Zhihui Fang is Professor of Education at the University of Florida, Gainesville, where he also coordinates the Reading Education program. He received a Ph.D. in language and literacy education from Purdue University. He studies content area reading and emergent literacy from a functional linguistics perspective and comes to this project from teacher education contexts where he has been engaged in helping secondary teachers teach reading in content areas. His research has been reported in *Reading Research Quarterly, Journal of Literacy Research, Linguistics and Education, International Journal of Science Education, Journal of Adolescent and Adult Literacy, Journal of Teacher Education*, and other publications. He is author (with Linda Lamme and Rose Pringle) of *Teaching Reading, Language, and Literature in Inquiry-Based Science Classrooms, Grades 4–8* (Christopher-Gordon, 2009) and editor of *Literacy Teaching and Learning: Current Issues and Trends* (Merrill/Prentice Hall, 2005).

Mary J. Schleppegrell is Professor of Education at the University of Michigan, Ann Arbor. She received a Ph.D. in linguistics from Georgetown University. Her research focuses on the language demands of schooling. She collaborated with the California History Project to develop a professional development program in *Literacy in History* for middle school and high school teachers who engage in functional grammar analysis to support the learning of English language learners and struggling readers. Author of *The Language of Schooling* (Erlbaum, 2004) and co-editor (with Cecilia Colombi) of *Developing Advanced Literacy in First and Second Languages: Meaning with Power* (Erlbaum, 2002), she has published her research in *Linguistics and Education, Research in the Teaching of English, Reading and Writing Quarterly, Journal of Literacy Research, TESOL Quarterly*, and other publications.

CONTRIBUTORS

Jingzi Huang is Associate Professor of Education at Monmouth University in West Long Branch, New Jersey. She earned her Ph.D. in language education from the University of British Columbia, Vancouver. She has taught in elementary, secondary, and university settings in Canada, China, and the United States. Her research explores classroom discourse, second and foreign language education, and literacy skills development in the content areas. Her work has appeared in the *International Journal of Applied Linguistics*, *Linguistics and Education*, *Language and Education*, *Language Culture and Curriculum*, *Language Teaching Research*, and *Communication Education*.

Annabelle Lukin is a Research Fellow and Lecturer in the Center for Language in Social Life, Department of Linguistics, Macquarie University, Sydney, Australia. Her chapter in this book was developed as a result of her Ph.D. research in linguistics at Macquarie that considered the teaching of poetry in the senior school through the analysis of curriculum documents, student essays, poems, and literary criticism. Her current research is on media discourse, focusing on Australian and international media coverage of the invasion and occupation of Iraq. Her other research interests include educational linguistics, political discourse, and language development and evolution. She is co-editor (with Geoff Williams) of *The Development of Language: Functional Perspectives on Species and Individuals* (Continuum, 2006), and her work has appeared in *Discourse and Society* and other publications.

Bruce Normandia is Associate Professor of Mathematics Education at Monmouth University in West Long Branch, New Jersey. He earned his Ed.D. in mathematics education from Rutgers University. He has taught high school mathematics, supervised mathematics instruction, and served as principal and superintendent of schools, with more than forty years of contributions to education in diverse contexts. His research explores the teaching of mathematics for conceptual understanding and the role language plays toward that end. His work has appeared in *Communication Education* and other publications.

INDEX